D1072193

EUGENE J. KELLEY, editor
The Pennsylvania State University

PRENTICE-HALL FOUNDATIONS OF MARKETING SERIES

PRENTICE-HALL FOUNDATIONS OF MARKETING SERIES

PRENTICE-HALL, INC., Englewood Cliffs, New Jersey

ORGANIZATIONAL
BUYING BEHAVIOR

FREDERICK E. WEBSTER, JR.
Amos Tuck School, Dartmouth College

YORAM WIND
University of Pennsylvania

ORGANIZATIONAL BUYING BEHAVIOR

FREDERICK E. WEBSTER, JR.
Dartmouth College

YORAM WIND
University of Pennsylvania

PRENTICE-HALL, INC., Englewood Cliffs, New Jersey

FOUNDATIONS OF MARKETING SERIES

Printed in the United States of America

Library of Congress
Catalog Card No.: 75-170040

ISBN: 0-13-640953-9

10 9 8 7 6 5 4 3 2 1

PRENTICE-HALL INTERNATIONAL, INC., *London*
PRENTICE-HALL OF AUSTRALIA, PTY. LTD., *Sydney*
PRENTICE-HALL OF CANADA, LTD., *Toronto*
PRENTICE-HALL OF INDIA PRIVATE LIMITED, *New Delhi*
PRENTICE-HALL OF JAPAN, INC., *Tokyo*

FOUNDATIONS
OF
MARKETING SERIES

The Foundations of Marketing is a series of authoritative and concise books prepared to serve the need for teaching materials incorporating the results of recent research and developments in the study and practice of marketing. The structure of the series—its flexibility within unity of purpose—enables the teacher to construct a complete basic marketing course, adjustable to a level of rigor of the teacher's choosing. Certain or all books can be combined to accomplish individual course objectives. Individual books are self-contained, reasonably complete treatments of the fundamental changes taking place in their areas. Students have the benefits of being introduced to the managerial approach to the field and to the socioeconomic process of marketing by authorities actively engaged in study and research in each field.

An overview of the series and of the managerial approach to marketing is provided by

Marketing Planning and Competitive Strategy

Four books treat important aspects of scientific methodology and decision making in marketing:

Consumer Behavior
Marketing Management and the Behavioral Environment
Men, Motives, and Markets
Quantitative Methods in Marketing

Key policy areas of marketing are covered in

Pricing Decisions in Marketing Policy
Product Policy and Strategy

Important environmental areas in marketing are emphasized in

All books may profitably use as supplements

It is hoped that the series will stimulate independent and intelligent thought about the central issues of marketing analysis and policy and that readers will find the books useful guides to a creative and disciplined approach to meeting complex and changing marketing problems.

EUGENE J. KELLEY, *Editor*

Despite the fact that the study of organizational buying behavior is in its fledgling stages, several marketing scholars have shared our interest in the subject. Among those who have been most helpful are Professors Richard Cardozo, University of Minnesota; Charles Goodman, University of Pennsylvania; Francesco Nicosia, University of California, Berkeley; and Lawrence Wortzel, Boston University. We wish to acknowledge with sincere thanks the important contributions they have made through their use and review of the materials presented here.

FREDERICK E. WEBSTER, JR.

YORAM WIND

FOREWORD

The purpose of business is to create a satisfied customer, and for many businesses the customer is a large organization rather than an individual. These large organizations are complex, and so are the processes that lead to buying decisions. Understanding the buying decision processes is essential to developing the marketing programs of companies that sell to organizations, or to "industrial customers" as they are commonly referred to, and is important to the community for the contribution it makes to the more effective working of the market mechanism.

Considerable study has been made of the buying behavior of the individual in his role as a consumer, but comparatively little work has been done on the buying behavior of the individual in his role as a member of an organization. Much of what has been done is either primarily concerned with group behavior as such and only incidentally deals with buying behavior, or it is fragmentary, dealing with particular aspects of market behavior.

Professors Webster and Wind make a valuable contribution in developing a general model for the study of organizational buying behavior that will be useful to students and practitioners alike. This is done through systematically reviewing and integrating the contributions of those who have studied various aspects of the subject. Their model of organizational buying behavior is a synthesis of established theories of organizational behavior. The model is then given substantive content by considering the influence factors included in the model and what effect they have on the behavior of those involved in making buying decisions.

The value of this work to the student lies in assembling and organizing what we know of organizational buying behavior and providing a model that indicates where further work needs to be done. Although the work admittedly leaves many questions unanswered, the practitioner will find the systematic analysis of those things that influence organizational buying behavior helpful in better understanding his customers and the things that influence their behavior. The chapter on implications for marketing strategy is particularly helpful in that it develops the relationship of the findings of behavioral science for practical action.

ELMER LOTSHAW
*Former President, American Marketing Association
and Manager, Corporate Marketing and Economic Research
Owens-Illinois, Inc.*

CONTENTS

8

IMPLICATIONS FOR
MARKETING STRATEGY   108

THE NATURE AND STUDY OF ORGANIZATIONAL BUYING BEHAVIOR

All formal organizations, such as business firms, governmental agencies, hospitals, educational institutions, and religious and political organizations must purchase goods and services to be used in the conduct of their affairs. Industrial concerns, for example, buy raw materials, components, equipment, and supplies to be used in manufacturing, maintenance, transportation, and other aspects of the firms' activities. Intermediate marketing organizations (retailers, wholesalers, and so forth) buy products for resale and equipment and supplies to be used in conducting the firm's activities. Institutions such as hospitals and universities must purchase equipment, supplies, fuel, and building materials as well as a wide variety of services necessary for the accomplishment of their purposes. Such basic activities as communication, which characterize all formal organizations, require many purchased products and services, such as typewriters, electricity, telephone services, office supplies, data processing services and equipment, reproduction equipment, and furniture. Buying is a basic activity for all formal organizations.

Buying is a complex process, not an instantaneous act. Buying involves the determination of the need to purchase products or services, communications among those members of the organization who are involved in the purchase or will use the product or service, information-seeking activities, the evaluation of alternative purchasing actions, and the working out of necessary arrangements with supplying organizations. Organizational buying is therefore a complex process of decision making and communication, which takes place over time, involving several organizational members and relationships with other firms and institutions. It is much more than the simple act of placing an order with a supplier.

Responsibility for organizational buying is often delegated to specialists within the organization. Buyers (or "purchasing agents") are usually assigned responsibility for only a limited part of the total organizational buying process—namely, the actual purchasing activity consisting of the identification and evaluation of alternative sources of supply and the administrative details involved in establishing working relationships with vendors of goods and services. Other aspects of the organizational buying process, such as the determination of the kind of materials or items to be purchased and the standards to be used in evaluating potential suppliers, are often the responsibility of other members of the organization, although there is considerable variation among organizations in the division of labor between the purchasing personnel and the other members of the organization.

Organizational buying behavior is therefore defined as *the decision-making process by which formal organizations establish the need for purchased products and services, and identify, evaluate, and choose among alternative brands and suppliers.* "Decision making" is used here to include information-acquisition and processing activities, as well as choice processes and the development of goals and other criteria to be used in choosing among alternatives.

The purpose of this book is to develop a conceptual framework within which specific buying situations may be analyzed, as well as to draw together several viewpoints and research findings about organizational buying. Our viewpoint is that of the marketing manager who must understand the workings of the organizational buying process if he is to design maximally effective marketing strategies for his organizational customers or potential customers. A decision to consider organizational buying in general, rather than industrial buying in particular, is based upon a conviction that the fundamental processes of information acquisition, analysis, and decision making are basically similar in industrial, institutional, and other formal organizational settings. Although buying motivations may differ depending upon whether the organization buys for resale, production, or usage, or upon whether the organization is primarily profit-motivated or budget-constrained, such distinctions can be analyzed within a general conceptual framework for the organizational buying processes.

Organizational Buying and Marketing Strategy

In adopting the marketing concept as a part of its business philosophy, modern industry has become increasingly sensitive to the central importance of thorough information about and understanding of the potential customer as the basic building block of effective and efficient marketing strategy. In a nutshell, the marketing concept as it exists today is a business philosophy that sees the fundamental purpose of the business as the creation of satisfied customers. Long-run profit is a measure of the extent to which the firm is successful in achieving this fundamental purpose. The responsibility of marketing management, according to this philosophy, is to interpret conditions in the marketplace and to coordinate and influence the direction of company operations so as to ensure that the company's offerings of products and services have the highest probability of satisfying customer needs. The marketing concept thus emphasizes marketing management's long-term responsibilities for adjusting the company's operations to the changing market. Previous definitions of the marketing function had emphasized short-term responsibility for influencing the nature of demand through selling and other promotional activities. The marketing concept, in contrast to this older sense of the marketing function, holds that promotion (personal selling, advertising, sales promotion, and publicity) can be conducted more efficiently to the extent that marketing management has been successful in developing both the "best" combination of products and services and a distribution system that can efficiently deliver those goods and services to customers.

Although documentary proof is hard to come by, it is generally agreed that business firms that sell to individual and household consumers typically have been quicker to accept the marketing concept than have firms whose customers are other firms, institutions, and other formal organizations. On the whole, manufacturers of consumer packaged goods have led in such areas as the development of new techniques of marketing research, innovations in marketing organization, and creative use of communication media.

A systematic review of the marketing literature, or an analysis of the references cited in any book on buyer behavior, will reveal no more than a few studies in which the buyers were industrial firms, intermediate marketing organizations, or other kinds of formal organizations. It has been estimated that by 1980 the total dollar volume of transactions among business firms (inter-industry transactions that are not reckoned in national income accounting) will exceed the Gross National Product of the United States.[1] There is thus every reason to believe that marketing managers in firms whose customers are formal organizations could benefit as well as their consumer-goods counterparts from a well developed body of knowledge about buyer behavior, if such a body of knowledge were available to them.

Why Study Organizational Buying Behavior?

All marketing strategy decisions involve the prediction of buyer behavior. When the marketing manager adjusts one of the variables under his control (product, price, promotion, and channel variables), he is at least implicitly making a prediction of market response.

The accuracy of these predictions of buyer response reflects both the adequacy of the market information available to the marketing strategist *and* the conceptual knowledge, or models, available to him for organizing and interpreting that information. A model is a set of assumptions or propositions about the operation of some system in nature. For the marketing manager, the relevant assumptions are those that pertain to the operation of the marketing system he is trying to influence with his marketing strategy. It has been said that "there is nothing so useful as a good model," and indeed "good" marketing managers—those with the best ratio of successful decisions to unsuccessful ones—are distinguished by their better predictions, based in part upon the adequacy of the model of the market process which they use (implicitly or explicitly) as a basis for both information gathering and predictions (assumptions) of the possible market response to their marketing strategies. The influence of the manager's models on development of strategies is illustrated in Figure 1–1.

The required conceptual knowledge for marketing managers whose customers are formal organizations can be based either on the traditional marketing and purchasing knowledge or on concepts and findings from the behavioral sciences. Basing conceptual knowledge on traditional marketing and purchasing information ignores to a large extent the existing knowledge that has been accumulated throughout the years in psychology, sociology, anthropology, communication, and the other behavioral sciences. This approach would be sound only if buying behavior is so different from other forms of human behavior that no theories and findings from the behavioral sciences are of any relevance. Since few would accept this assumption, there has been a tendency to base conceptual knowledge about marketing on concepts, theories, and findings from the behavioral sciences. The major limitations of this approach are that the findings are not based on marketing-related situations and variables and that there is no unified theory that can provide one clear and unambiguous explanation of human

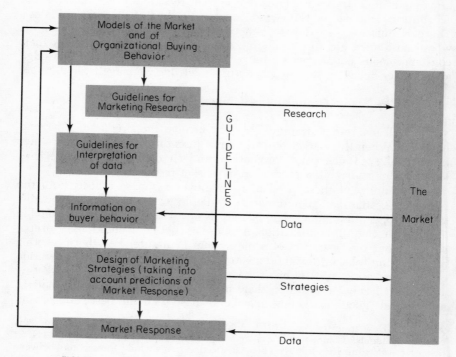

FIGURE 1–1. The Role of Models in Designing Marketing Strategies

behavior. Given the inadequacy of both of these approaches, what should be the role of behavioral science in constructing models of organizational buying behavior?

Although conceptual knowledge from the behavioral sciences seldom permits precise predictions and understanding of market response unless it is verified in a relevant marketing context, such knowledge does provide useful inputs to the design of relevant models within which one can assess the likelihood of different kinds and degrees of market response to alternative marketing actions. Most importantly, a familiarity with behavioral science concepts can help the marketing strategist take into account the most significant variables that are likely to determine response. It can sensitize him to the complexities of behavior. The answer to the question "What will happen if . . ." is usually "It depends." A theory of buyer behavior can be useful in defining those factors upon which market response "depends." [2]

In this sense, a model of organizational buying behavior based on the behavioral sciences has three major practical values for marketing personnel:

1. It can help identify, guide, and evaluate the need for market information—i.e., it can suggest which factors are most likely to affect the market's response to marketing effort, and hence which are worth gathering information about.

2. It can significantly aid in the analysis and interpretation of available information about the market, whether systematically gathered through marketing research or obtained in the normal conduct of business.

3. It can improve the value of predictions about and understanding of market response, hence improving the firm's marketing strategies toward the various organizational market segments.

The importance of conceptual knowledge (models) of buying behavior in understanding and predicting the possible response of the relevant market segments is widely accepted when the buyers are individuals and households; it is largely ignored, unfortunately, when the buying unit is an organization. Several factors may explain the lack of attention to organizational buying, including the basic complexity of organizational buying behavior. Some aspects of this complexity are evident from the characteristics of organizational buying behavior.

Some Characteristics of Organizational Buying Behavior

Organizations are continuously engaged in recurring cycles of problem-solving functions. The problem-solving function that has to be performed in organizational buying depends of course on the newness of the purchase task. In a new purchasing situation it is likely that the organization will go through all of the problem-solving stages, whereas in a straight rebuy some shortcut route will be undertaken.[3] But what are these problem-solving functions? As might be expected, there is no one generally accepted model of these various functions. The complexity of organizational buying behavior is illustrated by a semi-chronological model of the cycle of problem solving presented by Dr. Clawson in one of the early marketing seminars.[4] The twenty-four activities on Dr. Clawson's list are not unlike the functions of any target-seeking mechanism such as a household. In the organizational context, however, there are a number of added complexities.

First, and perhaps most important, organizational buying decisions are made more complex by the fact that more people usually are involved in them and different people are likely to play different buying roles. The roles of users, influencers, deciders, and buyers can be identified in most buying situations, and there are likely to be many people occupying each role—several influencers, decision-makers, users, and so forth. Furthermore, the persons occupying each role in a given organization are likely to change from one purchase situation to the next. Operationally, therefore, when dealing with organizational buying one should not be concerned only with the buyer (a member of the purchasing department) but with a *buying center*—that is, all those individuals and groups who participate in the purchasing decision-making process, who share some common goals and the risks arising from the decisions. A critical task for the marketer selling to organizations is to identify the members of the buying center, to determine their respective roles in the decision-making process, and to determine the criteria they will be using in their evaluations of alternative courses of buying action.

Second, organizational buying decisions often involve major technical complexities relating to the product or service being purchased. Technical evaluation of new equipment requires a great deal of factual information about the equipment as well as carefully studied opinions by those who can best predict the important new directions the technology is likely to take. Technical complexity is an important characteristic of many organizational purchasing situations, not just for equipment but for materials and for services as well.

Third, organizational buying decisions typically take longer to make than consumer (individual) buying decisions Because of the technical complexity involved in organizational buying, decisions require more information, undergo longer evaluations, and involve more uncertainty about product performance; evaluations are likely to be more complete because of the large amount of money involved, the complexity of the formal organization, and the fact that, once a relationship is worked out with a supplier, the organization becomes dependent upon that supplier for the day-to-day

[3] Patrick J. Robinson and Charles Faris, *Industrial Buying and Creative Marketing* (Boston: Allyn & Bacon, Inc., 1967).

[4] C. Joseph Clawson, "Problem Solving Functions in the Behavior of Business Firms," *Cost and Profit Outlook*, X, No. 10 (October 1957), 1–6.

conduct of its affairs. Purchased products and services are expected to contribute dependably to the organization's performance over long periods of time; as a result, the original decision is likely to be made in a cautious and thorough manner.

Fourth, the greater time required for organizational buying decisions means that there are significant lags between the application of marketing effort and obtaining a buying response. It is hard to tell whether a particular sales call or a specific service rendered for a potential organizational customer has produced any results. Not only does this contribute to the complexity of the marketing manager's task, but it also makes the study of industrial buying behavior a more difficult assignment.

Fifth, each buying organization is likely to be significantly different from every other buying organization in the potential market in ways that may require viewing each organization as a separate market segment. This is less true in consumer markets where a market segment may consist of a substantial number of individual units. Organizations are likely to vary significantly in the nature of the buying problems they face because their objectives, resources, people, and abilities are different. From the viewpoint of the marketing strategist whose customers are organizations, these differences must be taken into account in developing the marketing strategy to be used with each account. Few consumer goods companies must be so concerned about tailoring their marketing strategies to each individual consumer or household.

Finally, the organizational members participating in the buying function are neither purely "economic men" nor are their motives purely emotional and irrational. Rather they are human beings whose decisions and behavior are being influenced by both *task-* and *nontask*-related variables. The importance of this more realistic view of organizational buying behavior will be apparent in Chapter 3, when a model of organizational buying behavior will be proposed.

Organizational buying process is not only more complex than consumer buying behavior but also more complex than the process that leads to many other organizational decisions. This added complexity is primarily due to four factors:

1. The purchasing work flow is almost entirely crosswise in the organization rather than along the chain of command— i.e., most of the buyer's relations are horizontal relations with the users which are of about the same formal rank in the overall organizational hierarchy.

2. Formal authority over buyers can be in the hands of either a purchasing manager *or* an operating division manager (in the case of decentralization).

3. A major part of the buyer's work is with people outside the organization (vendors, salesmen, etc.).

4. Purchasing is a service function (auxiliary) and, especially in engineering-oriented organizations, the buyers have substantially lower status than the engineers in the using de-

partments. Yet, despite these status differences, no superior-subordinate relations exist between them, and thus, according to Sayles, "There are no clear-cut established deference patterns in which one of the parties is prepared to accept unequivocally the initiations for action of the others." [5]

As a first step, let us recognize the major determinants of organizational buying behavior as the environmental factors (including marketing inputs of various suppliers), the organizational characteristics, the interpersonal relationships among the members in the buying center, and the individual characteristics of these members. The focus of the analysis that follows is the buying center, those organizational members who are involved in the buying decision process. The marketer must define the buying center and systematically analyze the forces influencing its actions. This can be a difficult job because of the complexity of the organizational buying process; it can be aided by a conceptual understanding of the buying process. It is the purpose of this text to provide such an understanding—a view of the buying center as a set of organizational actors motivated by a complex interaction of personal and organizational objectives, operating within the limits of the technology, resources, and formal structure of the organization (including subsystems of authority, status, communication, rewards, and work flow). Although we should never forget that these organizational actors are individuals motivated by personal goals for gain and achievement, it is likewise important to determine the host of interpersonal, organizational, and environmental influences on their decision-making behavior.

Approaches to the Study of Organizational Buying Behavior

A model of organizational buying behavior can take one of two forms: (1) a stimulus-response type model which relates inputs (marketing stimuli) to output (buyers' response); or (2) a stimulus-respondent-response model which consists of a set of propositions about how the buyer responds to marketing stimuli, and may provide some generalizable answers about how inputs lead to outputs. The basic elements of these models are presented in simplified fashion in Figure 1–2.

Figure 1–2 can be called in general a "black box" model, to use a term that has appeared frequently in the marketing literature, because it sees the buyer as a "black box" into which one places certain inputs or stimuli and from which are emitted certain outputs or responses. The contents of the "black box" cannot be observed or measured directly but must be inferred from the observation of responses.

[5] L. R. Sayles, *Managerial Behavior and Administration in Complex Organizations* (New York: McGraw-Hill Book Co., Inc., 1964), p. 59.

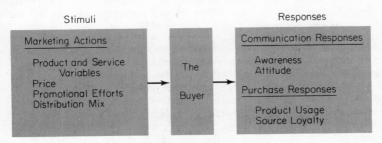

FIGURE 1–2. A Simplified Model of Buyer Response

This type of model is common to much of the behavioral sciences. To take a specific example, "motives" and "attitudes" are important elements in many theories of human behavior. These are hypothetical constructs developed to explain a relationship between observed responses and observed or controlled stimuli. Nobody has ever directly observed a motive or an attitude; rather, they must be inferred from observations of physical, physiological, and verbal behavior (opinions) of research subjects. Although based only upon inferences of causal relationships between stimuli and responses, these hypothetical constructs are nonetheless valuable as part of various models of buyer behavior or even in some cases as predictive and explanatory variables in their own right.

When one recognizes the complexity of organizational buying behavior, the large number of behavioral science and management findings and theories which can be utilized in explaining this form of behavior, and the multiplicity of the possible determinants of organizational buying behavior that include a complex interaction of individual, social, organizational, and environmental task and nontask factors, it becomes obvious that no one theory and no one area of behavioral science is likely to provide adequate insight into the nature of that process. It is virtually impossible to borrow a single conceptual framework, such as learning theory or role theory or organization theory, to analyze the organizational buying process. For this reason, the study of organizational buying behavior must have an *interdisciplinary focus* and must be eclectic in borrowing from whatever fields of behavioral and policy sciences are likely to help us understand the relationship between particular inputs and specific responses or buying actions.

Comprehensive models of consumer behavior such as the ones proposed by Nicosia,[6] Amstutz,[7] Engel, Kollat, and Blackwell,[8] and Howard and Sheth,[9] all have some relevance to the understanding of the buying decision processes followed by individuals within the context of formal organizations. Since they all leave out the influence of the formal organization, they should be modified if it is desired to use them as possible models of organizational buying behavior. Nicosia, for example, in summarizing his model describes a first approximation of the structure of the buying decision process as the following flow:

> The firm, its advertisement, the consumer's possible exposure to it, the interaction between the advertisement and the consumer's pre-dispositions operating or evoked at the time of exposure [Field 1], the possible formation of an attitude, the possible transformation of this attitude into a motivation [Field 2—search for and evaluation of means-end(s) relation(s)], the possible conversion of this moti-vation into an act of purchase [Field 3], and then back to the con-sumer's predispositions, and to the firm [Field 4—the feedback].[10]

Change the words *consumer* to *organizational buyers*, and *advertisement* to *any marketing input* in the above statement and you have a general structure of organizational buying behavior. Operationally, however, going beyond this level is not feasible—not for consumer behavior and not for organizational buying behavior. The diversity of approaches to consumer behavior reflects to a large extent our ignorance of the specific decision process that determines consumer behavior. Any researcher can probably fit any observed behavior to any model he subscribes to. The value of these models lies not in their suggesting a specific decision process but in their focusing on the importance of decision processes and the need to under-stand these processes and their interactions with other variables (deter-minants).

Any decision-process model of buyer behavior can potentially serve as a basic framework for an organizational buying behavior model. Yet, to be helpful to the marketing manager who is going to use the model, it has to be expanded to include explicitly the variables that affect organizational buying decisions. Among these variables, the organizational setting is of major relevance. One should therefore examine possible interdisciplinary approaches to the study of organizational behavior. A start in this direction is provided by the behavioral theory of the firm.[11] Although this theoretical framework was developed as a descriptive theory of the operations of profit-motivated firms, it is equally applicable to nonprofit organizations. Its assertions are sufficiently general to apply to virtually any formal or-ganization. The behavioral theory of the firm is attractive for the study of

[6] Francesco M. Nicosia, *Consumer Decision Processes* (Englewood Cliffs, N.J.: Prentice-Hall, Inc., 1966).

[7] Arnold E. Amstutz, *Computer Simulation of Competitive Market Response* (Cambridge, Mass.: The M.I.T. Press, 1967).

[8] J. F. Engel, D. T. Kollat, and R. D. Blackwell, *Consumer Behavior* (New York: Holt, Rinehart & Winston, Inc., 1968).

[9] John A. Howard and Jagdish N. Sheth, *A Theory of Buyer Behavior* (New York: John Wiley & Sons, Inc., 1969).

[10] Francesco M. Nicosia, "Advertising Management, Consumer Behavior and Simulation," *Journal of Advertising Research*, VIII (March 1968), 29–37.

[11] Richard M. Cyert and James G. March, *A Behavioral Theory of the Firm* (Englewood Cliffs, N.J.: Prentice-Hall, Inc., 1963).

organizational buying because it specifically recognizes the interaction among the four kinds of determinants—individual, social, organizational, and environmental—that we have identified as being important.[12] It considers the limits on human rationality in formal decision-making systems and recognizes the complex interactions of task and nontask variables. It concentrates on individual behavior in the organizational context as information is sought and evaluated as the basis for reducing uncertainties about the outcomes of alternative courses of action. In all respects, it provides a useful practical framework for the analysis of organizational buying behavior.

The Plan of the Book

In this book, organizational buying behavior is analyzed as the basis for strategic planning in marketing. In Chapter 2, alternative views of organizational buying behavior will be described and evaluated. Chapter 3 will present an operational model of organizational buying behavior. In an attempt to overcome the major limitations of consumer behavior models, this model is designed as a block model that identifies the major sets of variables affecting organization buying behavior and requires the marketing strategist to assess the variables operative in each specific situation and their interrelationships.

The four subsequent chapters analyze each of the major determinants of organizational buying behavior. Chapter 4 analyzes environmental effects, Chapter 5 organizational effects, Chapter 6 interpersonal determinants, and Chapter 7 assesses individual characteristics affecting the organizational buying process. Finally, Chapter 8 summarizes the implications of this analysis for marketing strategy.

The purpose of this book is to consider systematically the myriad of factors that influence the buying process, and the interrelationships among these variables. The ultimate purpose of this analysis is better decisions relating to the development of marketing strategies for those firms whose customers are business firms, institutions, governmental agencies, professional offices and firms, and other kinds of organizations.

[12] See Frederick E. Webster, Jr., "Modeling the Industrial Buying Process," *Journal of Marketing Research*, II, No. 4 (November 1965), 370–76, and Yoram Wind, "Applying the Behavioral Theory of the Firm to Industrial Buying Decisions," *The Economic and Business Bulletin*, XX, No. 3 (Spring 1968), 22–28.

2

ALTERNATIVE VIEWS OF ORGANIZATIONAL BUYING BEHAVIOR

The study of organizational buying behavior can be approached from several different viewpoints, depending upon the analyst's purpose and favored discipline. The available literature concerning organizational buying comes from a variety of areas with marketing, organizational behavior, purchasing, and economics providing the major concentrations of interest.

In this chapter we will explore several views of the organizational buying process. Each will be described and critically evaluated against the criteria of completeness, validity, and predictive reliability. Our objective is to assess the major research and journalistic traditions relevant to the study of organizational buying. Although the research studies and the models to be examined have been developed almost exclusively in the context of industrial buying behavior, they can be readily generalized to all buying organizations. For the most part, it can be assumed that profit-motivated behavior is analogous to budget-constrained objective-seeking behavior.

Organizational buying behavior models can be categorized as "task" or "nontask" models. Task models are those emphasizing task-related variables (such as price) whereas the nontask models include models that attempt to explain organizational buying behavior based on a set of variables (such as the buyer's motives) which do not have a direct bearing on the specific problem to be solved by the buying task, although they may be important determinants of the final purchasing decision.

In addition to this pure classification into task and nontask models, one has of course to recognize some possible combinations of task and nontask variables in a single complex model. The models reviewed in this chapter follow this threefold classification and are categorized as task, nontask, and complex models.

Task-Oriented Models

The literature of economics, purchasing, and to some extent marketing has concentrated upon the task variables in the organizational buying process. These models all suffer the disadvantages of incompleteness because of their failure to consider nontask variables as determinants of industrial buying behavior. It will be instructive to examine several task-oriented models because they are the most familiar to students of marketing and provide the basis for much strategic decision making in marketing management.

THE MINIMUM PRICE MODEL

The minimum price model, the simplest of all models of organizational buying behavior, can be traced to the economist. It is an attempt to explain the behavior of firms, rather than of individuals.

Because the firm is motivated to maximize its profits, and because it has little or no ability to influence the price obtained for its output in a nearly perfectly competitive market, the firm is forced to attempt to obtain all factors of production (land, labor, capital, and purchased products) at the lowest possible price and to achieve the most efficient methods of operation. It immediately follows from this simple model that the organizational buyer will purchase that version of a product he wants that is offered to him at the lowest total price. This price-minimizing model from the theory of the firm, or microeconomics, also assumes that the buyer has near perfect information about the alternatives available to him in the market. It further assumes that competing brands are reasonably close substitutes. If these conditions are met, it is relatively easy for the buyer to apply the lowest-price criterion.

This model can be effectively used to understand the purchase of certain commodities such as sand for use in glass manufacturing or wheat for use in food processing. These products are essentially undifferentiated except for standard differences in grades and there are only a few major sellers available to the potential buyer. In commodity markets, the buyer tries to minimize the total price paid to obtain products of specified quality.

THE LOWEST TOTAL COST MODEL

The lowest total cost model is essentially an elaboration on the minimum price model in which additional costs (other than initial purchase price) are recognized as significant. This model also assumes a goal of profit-maximization and a very well informed buyer. It adjusts initial purchase price to reflect additional costs of the product-in-use, including the "opportunity" costs associated with profit opportunities foregone because of such contingencies as failure of the supplier to provide reliable deliveries, problems with product quality, and the costs of poor technical service.

THE RATIONAL BUYER MODEL

As early as 1924, Copeland presented a model of industrial buying in terms of rational buying and patronage motives.[1] The rational buyer model saw the organizational buying process as a "rational" economic choice process. Although these or similar models are obviously over-simplifications as generalizable statements about organizational buying behavior and of little value as descriptive models, they still have their proponents.

THE MATERIALS MANAGEMENT MODEL

The materials management concept assigns the chief procurement executive responsibility for all activities associated with managing the flow of materials to and from manufacturing. The function of materials management is usually said to include the determination of quality and quantity and to emphasize the search for lowest costs as the prime objective of management. It should be stressed that it is a normative not a descriptive model. There is a moot question whether combining all cost related functions into one position of organizational responsibility and authority is a reasonable solution to the suboptimization problem.

THE RECIPROCAL BUYING MODEL

Another task-oriented model is the reciprocal buying model. Reciprocity is the practice of buying from suppliers on the condition that they, in turn, purchase the company's products. This is the formalized procedure by which companies purchase from their customers. In practice, reciprocity becomes a very complex administrative problem as formulas are developed for sharing the business among potential customer/suppliers and systems are developed for monitoring and controlling the volume of transactions, both buying and selling, with potential vendors who are also customers. In recent years, this practice has come under careful legal scrutiny, and it now appears that reciprocal dealing in many situations can be regarded as a practice that tends to restrict competition and is thus in violation of the anti-trust laws regulating interstate commerce.

THE CONSTRAINED CHOICE MODEL

The constrained choice model concentrates on the fact that most supplier selection decisions involve choosing from a limited set of potential vendors.

[1] Melvin T. Copeland, *Principles of Merchandising* (Chicago: A. W. Shaw Co., 1924).

Potential suppliers in this set are "in" while all other potential suppliers are "out." Constraints on the set of possible suppliers can be imposed by any member of the buying organization who has the necessary power, including finance, production, and engineering.

The source loyalty model assumes that inertia is a major determinant of buying behavior and stresses habitual behavior, the tendency to favor previous suppliers. There are a number of reasons why this is a reasonably good model. First, it recognizes that much organizational buying is routine decision making. Second, it is consistent with the observation that purchasing managers are busy people who try to establish relationships with vendors that are likely to be self-perpetuating and easily maintained. Third, it is consistent with the notion of "satisficing" as an alternative to maximization behavior. The satisficing postulate, a central part of the behavioral theory of the firm, maintains that much managerial decision making consists of the search for satisfactory rather than optimum solutions to problems.[2]

The existence of source loyalty has been well confirmed by studies of industrial purchasing behavior.[3] The evidence consistently suggests that it takes some kind of "shock" to jolt the organizational buying out of a pattern of placing repeat orders with a favored supplier or to extend the constrained set of feasible suppliers. A moment's reflection will suggest several reasons for this behavior, including the costs associated with searching for new suppliers and establishing new relationships, the fact that users are likely to prefer established sources, the relatively low risk involved in dealing with known vendors, and the likelihood that the buyer has established personal relationships that he values with representatives of the supplying firm. New suppliers are likely to be considered only when the buying situation has completely new elements to it or when a potential vendor's sales effort succeeds in convincing the buyer to redefine his buying problems, to set his goals higher, or to consider new ways of accomplishing the buying task.

Although the constrained choice model applies to a large segment of total organizational buying decisions, it is virtually devoid of insights into buying situations involving new sets of constraints. New constraints and new tasks require new solutions and new relationships with new vendors.

These six task-oriented models all concentrate on the economic aspects of organizational buying behavior. They emphasize the search for least-cost solutions to purchasing problems and such variables as purchase price and related costs. With the possible exception of the constrained choice model, they are essentially devoid of behavioral content. They assume implicitly that the characteristics of the individual decision maker, or the interactions among members of the buying organization, or the nature of the formal organization itself have little relevance in the actual outcome of

2 Richard M. Cyert and James G. March, A Behavioral Theory of the Firm (Englewood Cliffs, N.J.: Prentice-Hall, Inc., 1963).

3 Yoram Wind, "Industrial Source Loyalty," Journal of Marketing Research, VII (November 1970), 450–57; and Murray Harding, "Who Really Makes the Purchasing Decisions?" Industrial Marketing, LI (September 1966), 76–81.

the decision process. Clearly, this oversight makes these models incomplete as descriptions of buying behavior in formal organizations.

Nontask-Oriented Models

Nontask-oriented models introduce human beings into the description of organizational buying behavior. The task-oriented models just discussed suggest that the buying decision could be turned over to a computer for a calculation of the lowest total cost (or the lowest total price) solutions to the buying problem once the feasible set has been defined. They treat buying as a clerical function and marketing strategy as primarily a pricing and product offering problem. They do not suggest an active role for promotional strategy. Nontask-oriented models introduce noneconomic (some would call them "nonrational") factors into the situation.

THE SELF-AGGRANDIZEMENT MODEL

The self-aggrandizement model emphasizes the desire of the buyer to use his position in the organization as a means to enhance his own income by obtaining favors from potential vendors. The buyer either may request or simply may accept when offered gifts such as entertainment, dining, tickets to sports events, merchandise, or even cash.

There are two rather obvious problems with using this model as the basis for marketing strategy. First, it is probably valid only for situations where there is in fact little to differentiate the offerings (real or perceived) of one supplier from those of another, and such more or less "pure" commodity situations are relatively rare in organizational buying. Second, there is a significant risk to be taken if the offering of such personal inducements to buy can significantly offend the sensitivities of the professional buyer. Our judgment is that only a minority of purchasing officials will respond favorably to such tactics. Most would politely decline. Some would become furious, and the risk of that reaction is probably not worth taking.

THE EGO-ENHANCEMENT MODEL

Although many professional managers may be offended by an offer of financial rewards if they favor a certain supplier, few will take offense at statements or behavior which recognize their individuality and worth as human beings. The ego-enhancement model simply recognizes that the organizational buyer is an individual with a self concept that is as valuable to him as the next fellow's. Like the self-aggrandizement model, the ego-enhancement model is an attempt to incorporate "emotional" factors into the minimum price or lowest total costs models.

THE PERCEIVED RISK MODEL

The perceived risk model emphasizes the buyer's uncertainty as he evaluates alternative courses of action. Originally proposed as a way of looking at consumer behavior by Bauer,[4] it has been elaborated by Cox[5] and extended to the industrial buying situation by Levitt.[6] According to the perceived risk model, buyers are motivated by a desire to reduce the amount of perceived risk in the buying situation to some acceptable level, which is not necessarily zero. Perceived risk is a function of the buyer's uncertainty about the likelihood of occurrence of an event (which can be stated as a probability between one and zero that the event will occur) and the consequences associated with that event if it should occur.

Buyers may adopt several strategies for reducing the amount of perceived risk. One is to avoid a decision. Another is to remain loyal to existing suppliers. (Notice that the task-oriented model of source loyalty ascribes this phenomenon to the costs of change while the perceived risk model associates this behavior with the buyer's perceptions of uncertainty —two quite different explanations for the same result.) A third alternative is to gather and evaluate additional information. A fourth way of reducing perceived risk is to do business with well-known, reputable, established suppliers.[7]

Levitt's research illustrates the importance of source effect (that is, effects due to communicator credibility), a phenomenon well known from communications research, in the special case of industrial marketing.[8] One of the factors determining the amount of perceived risk in a given buying situation is the organizational buyer's self-confidence in the specific decision he is required to make, as well as his generalized self-confidence.

It is this relationship between the individual characteristics of the buyer and the amount of perceived risk in the buying situation that leads us to classify the perceived risk model as a nontask-oriented model. It is a model that relies heavily upon the nontask variables of the buyer's self-confidence and the *perceived* credibility of the communication source as variables which explain purchasing behavior.

[4] Raymond A. Bauer, "Consumer Behavior as Risk Taking," in R. S. Hancock, ed., *Dynamic Marketing for a Changing World* (Chicago: American Marketing Association, 1960), pp. 389–98.

[5] Donald F. Cox, *Risk Taking and Information Handling in Consumer Behavior* (Boston: Division of Research, Graduate School of Business Administration, Harvard University, 1967).

[6] Theodore Levitt, *Industrial Purchasing Behavior: A Study of Communications Effects* (Boston: Division of Research, Graduate School of Business Administration, Harvard University, 1965).

[7] *Ibid.*

[8] See Carl I. Hovland, Irving L. Janis, and Harold H. Kelley, *Communication and Persuasion: Psychological Studies of Opinion Change* (New Haven: Yale University Press, 1963), esp. Chapter 2, "Credibility of the Communicator," pp. 19–53.

THE DYADIC INTERACTION MODEL

The dyadic interaction model is similar to the ego-enhancement model in that both emphasize the personal relationship between the buyer and the salesman. While the ego-enhancement model sees the salesman as a source of ego-gratification for the buyer, the dyadic interaction model emphasizes the influence of role expectations. These expectations are functions of a specific interaction situation.

The dyadic interaction model was originally developed in a non-organizational context by Evans in his study of insurance salesmen.[9] He found that the probability of a sale was higher to the extent that the prospect and the salesman had similar characteristics. These objective characteristics were believed to be determinants of a set of role expectations for salesmen and, in general, a preference for a salesman who is "like me."

This model has been extended by Tosi, who found that the buyer's expectations for the salesman were indeed important, especially in determining whether future interactions occurred. On the other hand, Tosi's research did not find that role consensus between the buyer and the salesman concerning how each should play his role was, in fact, important.[10]

Each party enters the interaction with certain expectations for his own behavior, or role, and for the behavior of the other person. The buyer through his responses to selling effort determines the way the salesman will behave in the selling situation. The specific interaction situation is an important determinant of organizational buying behavior. But additional factors must also be considered.

THE LATERAL RELATIONSHIPS MODEL

Because the dyadic interaction model emphasizes the specific interaction between the buyer and the salesman, the lateral relationships model considers interactions among members of the buying group. The focus of this model is the purchasing agent, and the interactions examined involve others of more or less equal status within the organization in terms of position on the formal organization chart. These others include personnel in production scheduling, engineering, production, and related activities that depend upon performance of the purchasing function for their effectiveness. This model is, in effect, a behavioral look at the same kinds of considerations involved in the lowest total cost model. Since the lowest total cost model considered the joint costs involving different departments of the organization, the lateral relationships model examines the same departments in terms of their social behavior.

The lateral relationships model sees value analysis as a kind of job

[9] Franklin B. Evans, "Selling as a Dyadic Relationship—A New Approach," *American Behavioral Scientist*, VI (May 1963), 76–79.

[10] Henry L. Tosi, "The Effects of Expectation Levels of Role Consensus on the Buyer-Seller Dyad," *Journal of Business*, XXXIX (October 1966), 516–29.

enlargement in which the purchasing agent is motivated by a desire to obtain more power and status within the organization as well as to obtain more control over the variables determining his performance. It concentrates on the potential conflicts between purchasing and other organizational positions and it considers tactics used by the purchasing agent to reduce the power and influence of others within the organization.

These conflicts come about because decisions are made elsewhere in the organization that constrain the range of possible alternatives and the scope of the purchaser's responsibility with the result that he loses power and status internally. The purchasing agent therefore develops tactics for managing his lateral relationships with others in the organization in such a way as to enhance his own status and power. We will examine the lateral relationships model more completely in Chapter 6.

THE BUYING INFLUENCES MODEL

The buying influences model recognizes that several individuals and several role sets are involved in the organizational buying decision process. It stresses the importance to the marketer of identifying these individuals within the organization, whom we have called the buying center, and of understanding the relationships among them. The buying influences model, which has been proposed as a correction of the common tendency to concentrate attention on the purchasing agent, is based on a recognition of the purchasing agent's limited authority and responsibility.

The buying influences model is a useful model for reminding the analyst of the complexity of organizational buying decisions. By stressing the fact that organizational buying is, in fact, a process involving many parts of the formal organization, it serves as an appropriate caution against oversimplified models.[11]

On the other hand, with the exception of the "Reward-Balance" model that is described in Chapter 5, the buying influences models are virtually devoid of predictive content. Having noted that there are likely to be many influences, and having warned that the purchasing agent is likely to have relatively little formal authority for setting specifications, the model then urges the analyst to dig deeper without providing any significant clues as to regularities or causal relationships among the several factors that define organizational buying decisions.

THE DIFFUSION PROCESS MODEL

The diffusion process model goes even further in broadening the view of buying decisions to include factors other than the purchasing agent. The diffusion process model views the firm as being located in a social system

---

[11] For just one example of the literature advocating the buying influences model, see Robert E. Weigand, "Why Studying the Purchasing Agent is Not Enough," *Journal of Marketing*, XXXII (January 1968), 41–45.

through which new products are "diffused" over time. The firm can be described in terms of its propensity to adopt new products and services at various stages in this process. The model suggests that there are certain characteristics of the firm which may determine whether it is early or late in accepting new products in the market, but it has little to say about the process by which such decisions are made. The firm is viewed essentially as a passive member of the social system.[12]

The diffusion process model is quite consistent with the perceived risk model, except that the former considers the firm as the decision-making unit whereas the perceived risk model focuses on the individual.

Task versus Nontask Models

Models that emphasize nontask variables such as role expectations or formal authority for purchasing tend to lose sight of the basic fact that work is being done in pursuit of the objectives of the buying organization. The fact that organizational buying is a form of problem-solving behavior is obscured in these models and the essential nature of the buying task is not given sufficient prominence.

Each of the foregoing task and nontask models has concentrated primarily on one set of variables to the exclusion of others. Each illuminates a portion of the organizational buying process for our viewing and leaves other parts in darkness. Even when all of these models are brought to bear simultaneously, there are still many dark spots, especially where important relationships and interactions among sets of variables provide unique dimensions to the buying process. To illuminate these parts of the process we need a complex comprehensive model, one which considers several sets of relevant variables.

Ideally, our model of the organizational buying process would include individual, group, organizational, and environmental variables and both task and nontask considerations. Furthermore, the ideal model would be based on empirical data and would have high validity and predictive reliability. No available model meets all of these criteria, but there are at least four "complex" models of the organizational buying process that do consider several sets of task and nontask variables simultaneously.

Complex Models

Complex models consider more than one variable or set of variables as factors influencing organizational buying responses to marketing effort. It should be stressed that complexity *per se* is not a virtue; the best model is always the simplest that permits a specified degree of predictive

---

[12] For an application of the diffusion model, with some extensions, to industrial buying, see Frederick E. Webster, Jr., "New Product Adoption in Industrial Markets: A Framework for Analysis," *Journal of Marketing*, XXXIII (July 1969), 35–39.

reliability and descriptive validity. Unfortunately, organizational buying is a complex process and single variable models are incapable of yielding the desired degree of validity and reliability.

THE DECISION PROCESS MODEL

The decision process model was implicit in our comments in Chapter 1 when we defined organizational buying as a complex process of decision making and communication which takes place over time, involving several organizational members and relationships with other organizations. More formally, the decision process model sees decision making as a five-stage process: (1) problem recognition; (2) identification of alternatives; (3) evaluation of alternatives; (4) selecting a course of action; and (5) implementation. This view emphasizes the time dimension and at least opens the door for consideration of individual, social, organizational, and environmental influences at each stage of the process.

The behavioral theory of the firm condenses decision making into two interdependent activities of search and choice. Search procedures include both identification and evaluation of alternatives as well as problem definition and the search for clarification of decision criteria. Choice procedures involve both individual and group processes for selecting among alternatives. One decision process model of organizational buying uses these concepts from the behavioral theory of the firm and divides the buying process into four phases:

1. *Problem recognition*—the creation of a buying situation through perception of a discrepancy between desired goals and actual performance. Goal-setting and problem-recognition are said to be influenced by both personal (i.e., individual, group, and organizational) and impersonal (i.e., organizational and environmental) factors.

2. *Assignment of buying authority and responsibility*—a combination of formal (organizational) and informal (interpersonal) processes by which the role sets of organization members are negotiated and defined. Considerations of formal organizational structure (degree of centralization) interact with technological, task-related factors and interpersonal considerations of status and power to define the buying group.

3. *Search process*—more or less routine procedures used by organizational members for obtaining information to be used in setting goals, identifying alternatives, and establishing selection criteria in the buying process. Search is constrained by both time and cost considerations and by the decision-maker's previous experience.

4. *Choice process*—the procedure for selecting among alternatives. This stage of the decision process may involve sev-

eral individuals and several distinct (and potentially conflicting) sets of criteria.[13]

This model obviously is "complex" in that it incorporates both task and
nontask variables and individual, social, organizational, and environmental
factors. As a general, descriptive model it has low predictive reliability,
however. The major weakness of this and other descriptive models is that
they are too general to serve as analytical tools for specific buying or
marketing situations. They provide an inadequate framework for specify-
ing the variables and relationships that must be studied in a particular
instance in order to predict buying actions.

THE COMPACT MODEL

The Competence-Activity (COMPACT) model was developed by Robinson and Stidsen [14] as a basis for both descriptive and normative analysis
of individual behavior in the context of an organizational framework. The
model, according to the authors, "shows the general relationship between
the phases of a system of action and the competence levels at which interactions may be analyzed. Each of the competence levels represents a 'layer'
of orientations of the acting system towards its situation and simultaneously represents a more or less explicit set of relational or communicative
capacities." [15] The model, illustrated in Figure 2–1, is based on three major
dimensions: (1) the activities of industrial purchasing decisions, which
include awareness (problem definition, allocation of resources, and decision to buy), acquisition (selection of suppliers and purchase), goal seeking (application or use of product or service), harmonization (assessment
of product and supplier performance), and commitment to product and/or
supplier; (2) the five levels of organizational scope of planning and decision making, which include the doer, supervisor, operating management,
integrative management, and top management, each with its own role,
from the doer's determination of the procedural "how to do it" guidelines
to top management's determination of strategic objectives; (3) the five
levels of individual motivational orientation or competence, ranging from
physical activity through adaptive behavior, instrumental performance, and
system integration, and values integration.

Conceptually, the model is quite appealing because it integrates the
sequence of decisions comprising a given purchase with the various organizational and individual characteristics which affect the purchase decisions.
Practically speaking, however, the COMPACT model is too abstract and
not very useful as an operational model of organizational buying behavior.

---

[13] Frederick E. Webster, Jr., "Modeling the Industrial Buying Process,"
Journal of Marketing Research, II (November 1965), 370–76.

[14] Patrick J. Robinson and Bent Stidsen, *Personal Selling in a Modern Perspective* (Boston: Allyn & Bacon, Inc., 1967).

[15] *Ibid.,* 105–6.

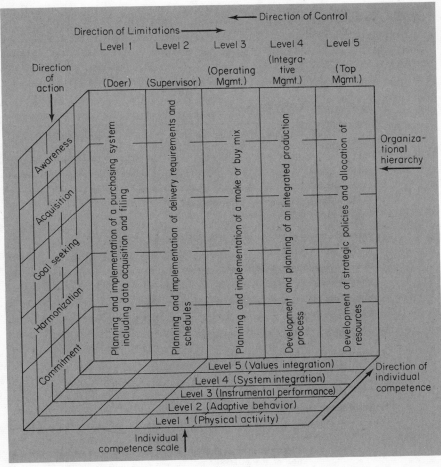

FIGURE 2–1. The Compact Model: A Three-Dimensional Model of the Buying System in the Context of the Firm

Reproduced, with permission, from Patrick J. Robinson and Bent Stidsen, Personal Selling in a Modern Perspective (Boston: Allyn & Bacon, Inc., 1967), p. 113.

THE BUYGRID MODEL

A descriptive study by the Marketing Science Institute concluded that an eight-stage model best described the organizational buying process. This analysis also concluded, however, that it was necessary to distinguish among three classes of buying situations inasmuch as the decision process showed significant differences depending upon whether it was a new task, modified rebuy, or straight rebuy situation. The resulting model, the BUY-GRID analytical framework, is shown in Table 2–1.[16]

Being empirically based, the BUYGRID framework provides a useful set of categories for classifying buying behaviors and organizational buying responses to marketing efforts. It has a number of significant implications for the design of marketing strategies, yet it is virtually devoid of predic-

TABLE 2–1. The BUYGRID Model

BUYPHASES	BUYCLASSES		
	New Task	Modified Rebuy	Straight Rebuy
1. Anticipation or Recognition of a problem (Need) and a General Solution			
2. Determination of Characteristics and Quantity of Needed Item			
3. Description of Characteristics and Quantity of Needed Item			
4. Search for and Qualification of Potential Sources			
5. Acquisition and Analysis of Proposals			
6. Evaluation of Proposals and Selection of Supplier(s)			
7. Selection of an Order Routine			
8. Performance Feedback and Evaluation			

Notes:
1. The most complex buying situations occur in the upper left portion of the BUYGRID matrix, when the largest number of decision makers and buying influences are involved. Thus, a New Task in its initial phase of problem recognition generally represents the greatest difficulty for management.
2. Clearly, a New Task may entail policy questions and special studies, whereas a Modified Rebuy may be more routine, and a straight rebuy essentially automatic.
3. As Buyphases are completed, moving from phase I through phase 8, the process of "creeping commitment" occurs, and there is diminishing likelihood of new vendors gaining access to the buying situation.

Reproduced, with permission, from Patrick J. Robinson, Charles W. Faris, and Yoram Wind, Industrial Buying and Creative Marketing (Boston: Allyn & Bacon, Inc., 1967), p. 14.

[16] Patrick J. Robinson, Charles W. Faris, and Yoram Wind, *Industrial Buying and Creative Marketing* (Boston: Allyn & Bacon, Inc., 1967).

tive ability, and offers little insight into the nature of the complex inter-play between task and nontask variables. The BUYGRID framework does not permit inferences about behavioral cause-and-effect relationships of the kind needed for designing efficient marketing strategies. Although these are serious criticisms, the complex BUYGRID model does have the virtue of completeness in the sense that individual, social, organizational, and environmental factors can all be positioned within this broad context. Furthermore, the model does provide guidelines for research but it tends to obscure important nontask variables such as status drives and role set conflicts.

SIMULATION MODELS

Simulation models extend the decision process models by permitting analysis of the impact of changed parameter values and of the relationships among variables over time. The general purpose of a simulation of the organizational buying process is to improve understanding of the performance and characteristics of the system and its responses to marketing stimuli. This better understanding can suggest better marketing strategies as well as more efficient buying organizations and procedures. At least one industrial firm has developed a computer-based simulation model of its own buying process with the purpose of using the computer for routine buying decisions. This study was not made public, however.

To the best of our knowledge, the only published report of a simulation of organizational buying is based on the BUYGRID model.[17] Using a modified version of the BUYPHASE (decision stages) process, the simulation contains four submodels:

1. A model for the evaluation of preassigned suppliers.
2. A model for the development of a set of feasible suppliers.
3. A model for the selection of suppliers under a straight rebuy situation.
4. A model for the selection of suppliers under a modified rebuy or new task situation.

Figure 2–2 shows the major steps in the BUYGRID simulation.

Simulation models offer the analyst the unique advantage of being able to ask "What will happen if . . . ?" questions by changing system parameter values and tracing the consequences of change. For the analysis of complex systems, simulation can be a powerful tool for extending the logical and analytical skills of the investigator. It must be remembered, however, that the results of a simulation of the organizational buying process (or any behavioral system) are no better than the underlying behavioral model on which it is based.

[17] Yoram Wind and Patrick J. Robinson, "Simulating the Industrial Buying Process," in Robert L. King, ed., *Marketing and the New Science of Planning* (Chicago: American Marketing Association, 1968), 441–48.

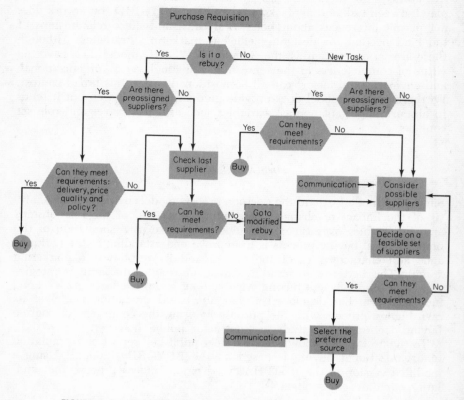

FIGURE 2–2. The Major Stages in the BUYGRID Simulation

Reproduced, with permission, from Patrick J. Robinson, Charles W. Faris, and Yoram Wind, Industrial Buying and Creative Marketing (Boston: Allyn and Bacon, 1967), p. 48.

The BUYGRID simulation was in a crude stage at the time it was reported and had little predictive ability. As we saw earlier, the basic model has several weaknesses and is too general to permit meaningful analysis of any specific buying organization or selling situation. The simulation nonetheless illustrates the feasibility of developing simulation models of the organizational buying process. Simulation continues to hold promise for both research and strategic planning applications.

Summary: Need for an Integrated Model

Available models for the most part overlook either task or nontask variables and are therefore inadequate analytical tools. An integrated model is required if we are to have sufficient understanding of the organizational buying process as the basis for marketing strategy. It must recognize the complex interaction of task and nontask variables and of individual, group, organizational, and environmental factors in determining response to marketing effort. It must also recognize the alternative forms of buying response and the sequential nature of the organizational buying decision process. Simple models such as the reciprocal buying model or the lowest total cost model as the basis for strategy are likely to produce disappointing results in most situations because many relevant factors are not subjected to careful scrutiny. The models examined in this chapter are not without value, however. Each illuminates a part of the total process and thus contributes to our understanding.

3

AN ORGANIZATIONAL BUYING BEHAVIOR MODEL

The complexity of organizational buying behavior reflects the many factors that influence the outcome of the organizational buying decision process. In this chapter we will develop a general model of organizational buying behavior that recognizes the complex interactions of task and nontask variables and of individual, group, organizational, and environmental factors in determining the buying responses to marketing efforts. It is our hope that this model will sketch out the conceptual territory and boundaries of organizational buying behavior in an integrative way.

The Model

The buying process in a formal organization usually involves several persons. Their decisions are influenced by other persons, by the organizational setting within which they operate, by the environmental constraints within which they and the organization perform, and by their individual characteristics. These multiple influences on the buying decisions can be expressed by the following equation:

$$B = f\ (I,G,O,E,)$$

which is just a different way of saying, "Buying behavior (B) is a function of individual characteristics (I), group factors (G), organizational factors (O) and environmental factors (E)."

Each of these four factors can influence the buying decisions through a set of variables relating to the buying "task," and/or through a set of variables not directly related to the task at hand.

Distinguishing between the task and nontask elements of the individual, group, organization, and environmental variables that affect the buying decisions suggests the following equation:

$$B = f\ (I_T,\ I_{NT},\ G_T,\ G_{NT},\ O_T,\ O_{NT},\ E_T,\ E_{NT})$$

where T stands for task variables and NT for nontask variables. A simple illustration of each of these eight variables is presented in Table 3–1.

TABLE 3–1.   A Classification of Determinants of
Organizational Buying Behavior

Source of Influence	Task Variables	Nontask Variables
Individual Factors	Desire to obtain lowest price	Personal values
Interpersonal (Social) Factors	Meetings to set product specifications	Off-the-job interactions among company employees
Organizational (Formal) Factors	Company policies with respect to product quality	Company policies regarding community relations
Environmental Factors	Expected trends in business conditions	Political factors in an election year

Given these eight sets of possible determinants of organizational buying behavior, the question becomes one of how they affect organizational buying behavior. Many of the existing models of organizational buying behavior have demonstrated that one variable, or at most a few variables, had some effect on organizational buying decisions. Unfortunately, most investigators stopped at this point. The process through which these variables affect organizational buying decisions, the strength of the relationships, the usefulness of the findings to marketing strategy, and, even more fundamentally, the precise conceptualization of the variables and their interrelations to other possible determinants of organizational buying behavior have often been lacking.

The model is basically an elaboration of the simple black box model presented in Figure 1–2. It is centered around the decision process carried out by the members of the buying center, and takes into account the various determinants of the decision. A schematic presentation of the model is illustrated in Figure 3–1.

The following sections will describe briefly the organizational decision process, the four pairs (task and nontask) of possible sets of determinants of the buying decisions, marketing strategies affecting the buying process, and the buying responses of the organization.

The Organizational Buying Decision Process

The organizational decision-making process, which is the core of the organizational buying process, is a complex process that takes place

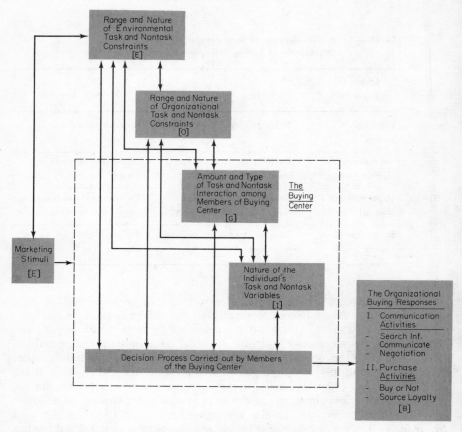

FIGURE 3–1. A Model of Organizational Buying Behavior

over time and involves several members of the given organization and relationships with other organizations. Whereas it is easy to describe the
decision process as the whole process leading to the various buying decisions, there are many different views of the number, nature, and sequence
of the various stages comprising it.

Webster, it will be recalled from Chapter 2, viewed the decision process
as consisting of four stages: problem recognition → assignment of buying
authority and responsibility → search process → and choice process.[1] The
Marketing Science Institute's study [2] presented the following eight stage

[1] Frederick E. Webster, Jr., "Modeling the Industrial Buying Process,"
Journal of Marketing Research, II (November 1965), 370–76.

[2] Patrick J. Robinson and Charles W. Faris, *Industrial Buying and Creative
Marketing* (Boston: Allyn & Bacon, Inc., 1967).

decision process: anticipation or recognition of a problem and a general solution → determination of characteristics and quality of needed item → description of characteristics and quantity of needed item → search for and qualification of potential sources → acquisition and analysis of proposals → evaluation of proposals and selection of supplier(s) → selection of an order routine → performance feedback and evaluation.

Despite the intuitive appeal and scattered evidence in favor of these somewhat similar descriptive models, there is no way to identify the one "true" decision-making process that exists in all organizational buying decision processes. Furthermore, it is most likely that such a universal decision-making process does not exist—primarily because of differences in organizational characteristics, the people who are involved in the various stages, the given buying situation, and the importance of the given task.

These and other differences suggest that every organization might have an idiosyncratic set of buying decision processes, which again might vary from one purchase situation to another. If this is the case, it seems that attempts to identify a *general* decision-making process are bound to be fruitless. It is for this reason that the organizational buying behavior model (Figure 3–1) includes a decision process without any attempt to identify the specific stages of the process. One should recognize, however, that the decision process is not merely the final act of choice among alternative courses of action, but is rather, as Simon points out, the whole process of finding occasion for making a decision, finding possible courses of action, and choosing among them.[3]

The organizational buying decision process can be described in terms of a general model of organizational decision processes composed of five basic stages, as shown in Figure 3–2. The specific nature, importance of, and

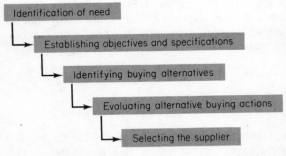

FIGURE 3–2. General Model of Organizational Decision Processes

interrelations among these stages vary across organizations and buying situations, yet this model does provide a good starting point for the understanding of the buying decision process.

3 Herbert A. Simon, *The New Science of Management Decision* (New York: Harper & Row, Publishers, Inc., 1960).

IDENTIFICATION OF NEED

It will be recalled from Chapter 1 that a buying situation is created when some member of the organization perceives a problem that can be solved through the purchase of a product or service. The perception of a buying problem can occur at any place in the organization and at almost any stage in the work of the organization.

ESTABLISHING OBJECTIVES AND SPECIFICATIONS

Eventually, the need for purchased goods and services will be defined with sufficient clarity to permit the drawing up of specifications for the purchase. Those who originally defined the buying need may or may not be involved in the establishment of specifications. Specifications grow directly out of the definition of the buying problem, which identifies certain objectives that the purchase must meet.

IDENTIFYING BUYING ALTERNATIVES

When the specifications and schedules for the purchase have been defined, at least in preliminary fashion, the market is searched for available alternatives. Previously used sources of information and sources of supply will be consulted first. Depending upon the nature of the buying problem, several organizational members may be involved in the identification of buying alternatives. The purchasing department will obviously be involved. In addition, engineering people (especially in manufacturing companies) are likely to provide inputs to this stage of the buying decision as well.

EVALUATING ALTERNATIVE BUYING ACTIONS

The evaluation of alternative buying actions is the key step in the buying decision process. In rudimentary form, it consists of comparing the characteristics of the available alternatives against the criteria established when specifications and schedules were set. This is an easy process only in the relatively straightforward case of simple, unambiguous specifications with virtually identical alternatives that vary with respect to only one central determining feature such as price. When a standard commodity that is easily graded is being purchased, it is possible to request competitive bids and to award the purchase to the lowest bidder. Seldom are things so simple.

In the more common situation, the available alternatives will differ significantly from one another. Some will have features that are not available with others, or it will not be clear how closely each of the alternatives meets the specifications that have been established, or there will be some uncertainty about the ability of the various sources of supply to meet the schedules that have been established.

To resolve these ambiguous decision situations, it is necessary to weight some criteria (i.e., specifications) more heavily than others. It must be decided, for example, whether price or product quality is a more important variable and the appropriate tradeoffs among product quality features must be established. Also to the extent that different persons are involved in the buying decision process and are likely to employ different criteria in their evaluations, conflict is going to occur among members of the buying group.

SELECTING THE SUPPLIER

In situations where single criteria cannot be applied and where there is disagreement about the ability of various potential suppliers to meet the specifications, the final decision about suppliers may reflect the relative power and influence of the various members of the buying group. Formal authority for the purchase decision may belong to the purchasing agent but his actual authority may be limited.

To summarize, the buying decision process, as it occurs over time, can be described by several stages: identification of need, establishing specifications, identifying buying alternatives, evaluating alternative buying actions, and selecting the supplier. These are not clearly defined stages but rather steps in a continuous process. Some steps may be repeated several times and there may be much "recycling" within the basic process, as when new specifications are defined after an initial evaluation of alternatives or when new sources of information are consulted in the evaluation stage.

This description of the buying decision process is oversimplified and ignores the large number of decisions that may occur at each decision stage (i.e., deciding how to generate alternatives, how many to seek, etc.). Further complexity is derived from the fact that the buying decisions are being made and carried out by a number of organizational members who fulfill the roles of decision-makers, influencers, and gatekeepers with respect to the various usage and buying decisions.

FACTORS INFLUENCING BUYING DECISIONS

As stated in the model, buying decisions are influenced by four interacting sets of factors: environmental, organizational, interpersonal, and individual. Furthermore, these variables can be dichotomized as either "task" (those that are directly related to the organizational buying problem as defined by the organizational objectives) or "nontask" (those that are not directly related to the buying problem).

Environmental Factors. The organization itself, its members, and the patterns of interaction among them are all subject to certain environmental influences. The task versus nontask distinction is relevant for understanding these influences. Task-related environmental forces are primarily those derived from inter-organizational relations. Of utmost importance among these relationships are the marketing stimuli presented by prospective suppliers. The task-related environmental influences are not limited, however, to institutions, but also embrace the specific technical, political, and economic characteristics of the society within which the buying organization operates insofar as they affect the buying task.

Nontask-related environmental factors include both the influence of other organizations and the general social-cultural-political environment. Among the institutions that have no direct task relations with the focal organization are various social institutions, the government, and facilitating business organizations such as banks, transportation companies, and the like, which are an integral part of the environment within which any organizational buying decisions take place. In addition to these nontask-related institutions, the values of any given society exert significant influence on the organizational buying process. Since organizational buying is basically the result of the actions and decisions of individuals, the values of these individuals consciously or unconsciously affect their buying decisions.

Organizational Factors. The formal organization itself has many task and nontask dimensions which significantly influence the buying decision-making process. Objectives, policies, procedures, structure, and systems of rewards, authority, status, and communication define the formal organization as an entity and significantly influence the buying process at all stages.

It is the objectives of the formal organization which, in the first instance, define the existence of a buying situation. Products and services are purchased to facilitate goal accomplishment. A buying "problem" is defined by a discrepancy between the level of goal attainment perceived to be desirable and the level expected to exist if no action is taken. Alternative courses of action can be evaluated according to their ability to contribute to the accomplishment of the organization's goals.

Once again, the distinction between task- and nontask-related factors is found to be relevant. In a given buying situation, the organizational factors that are directly related to the buying task include organizational policies providing specific criteria as to the kind of material to be purchased and the specifications for product quality that must be met. Other task-related organizational factors include the technical requirements created by the nature of the organization's operations (such as production equipment constraints) and time-related variables such as delivery requirements and the number of days' worth of inventories that must be maintained.

Organizations also have a set of policies that relate to purchasing activity, but on an indirect, nontask basis. For example, the Federal Government attempts to use its enormous defense spending in such a way as to also further important social objectives, as by favoring vendors in depressed labor market areas. In other organizational settings, nontask policies that might be reflected in purchasing activities include the favoring of local businesses and preferences for dealing with suppliers who are also customers (reciprocity), to name only two. The formal structure of the organization, including its systems for rewarding performance, for assigning status and power to individuals, and for communication, can significantly determine the nature of buying actions.

The status and power system operates in similar fashion to introduce a series of nontask-related factors into the buying decision-making process. Influencers may have more status and power than deciders or buyers. Technology-based organizations often assign high status to individuals who have been trained in the physical sciences and engineering and therefore give these individuals a great deal of power in decision making in general, including purchasing.

Likewise, the structure for the transfer of information among organizational members can exert a direct and significant influence on the outcome of the purchasing decision. Regularly scheduled committee meetings may be the vehicle for discussing buying problems, and vendors wishing to be considered in a buying situation may be required to make presentations to that committee on a certain date, with failure to do so precluding the firm from further consideration. The specific composition of such committees also may exert significant influence on the outcome of these discussions.

Interpersonal Factors. The buying process in a formal organization usually involves several persons. These persons interact on the basis of their particular roles in the buying process—as influencers, users, deciders, buyers, and gatekeepers (who control the flow of information into the buying group)—as well as on the basis of the history of the group's previous interactions and social experiences. The buying group is characterized by both a pattern of communication (interaction) and a set of shared values (norms) which direct and constrain the behavior of the individual within it.

The notion of the "buying center" is of major significance in the study of buying behavior in formal organizations. The "buying center" is defined as consisting of those individuals who interact for the specific purpose of accomplishing the buying task. As indicated above, the buying center may consist of individuals occupying any of the followng roles—deciders, influencers, buyers, users, and gatekeepers.

Deciders have formal authority and responsibility for deciding among alternative brands and vendors. Influencers do not necessarily have buying authority but can influence the outcome of the decision through the application of constraints. Buyers have formal authority for selecting vendors and consummating the buying decision. This formal authority may be significantly constrained, however, by the influence of organizational members who occupy other, more powerful roles in the buying group. Users are those who actually use the purchased products and services but who may have little or no buying authority and varying amounts of buying influence. Gatekeepers control the flow of information into the buying group. This function is often performed by secretaries who screen mail or telephone calls, librarians who determine what may be read, and, most importantly, by the purchasing agent who has formal authority to control the activities of salesmen who call upon others in the organization; he can deny permission to a salesman to call upon an influencer or a user and thus, through his "gatekeeping" activities, can exert a subtle, indirect influence on the buying process.

The buying center thus is defined in part by social activity relating to task performance. Similarly, roles in the buying center are defined in terms of the buying task. It must be recognized, however, that interaction among members of the buying center is also significantly influenced by other roles and social factors which extend beyond the buying task.

The outcome of interactions among members of the buying group is determined by the interaction of task and nontask variables and reflects the simultaneous performance of several roles by the members. One individual may occupy the roles of user and decider, or of buyer and gatekeeper, or of influencer and buyer, as well as other, nontask roles that influence his behavior, such as the roles of professional manager, Republican, and father. Promotional effort by potential suppliers can be directed at each of these roles.

Individual Factors. Although organizational buying is the result of organizational decision making, individual behavior defines this decision-making system. Each person involved in the buying process brings to it a set of needs, goals, habits, past experiences, information, attitudes, and so on which he applies in each specific situation. Some of these factors can be classified as task variables. Others, such as the company president's wish to favor his brother-in-law's firm as a supplier, may be nontask variables. The task versus nontask distinction does not necessarily imply goal conflict.

The behavior of individuals in formal organizations is a complex interaction of personal, group, and organizational goal-seeking behaviors. Although all behavior is motivated by the needs of individuals and their search for individual satisfactions, organization members also accept and strive for the accomplishment of the goals of their groups and their organization. When an individual occupies a position in a formal organization, he implicitly accepts the notion that he and the organization can work together to achieve their distinct objectives. Thus the individual accepts the objectives of the organization as his own while also deciding that the organization represents the best opportunity to pursue his own objectives and satisfy his own needs.

Individual factors of importance in organizational buying include the individual's age, income, education, professional identification, personality, and other psycho-socioeconomic characteristics. Another set of individual factors, probably more important, is represented by the individual's predispositions, including awareness, attitudes, and preferences, toward specific suppliers and their brands. Other variables of significance relate to the individual's characteristic methods of searching for information and of processing the information available to him concerning alternative sources of supply. Related to information processing are such individual characteristics as self-confidence and ability to tolerate uncertainty and risk.

SUPPLIERS' MARKETING INPUTS INTO THE ORGANIZATIONAL BUYING PROCESS

Although they constitute part of the environmental factors, the marketing strategies of the firms attempting to market their products and services to the buying organization deserve special attention because they are the major controllable variables which the supplying firm can change and manipulate at will.

Members of the organization buying center and especially the buyers (members of the purchasing department) are subjected to an ever increasing influx of input from various sources. These inputs aimed at the buying organization are the final outcome of the carefully designed marketing strategies of competing sources of supply. The strategies, which include product and service, promotion and distribution, are aimed at influencing the buyers and decision-makers to purchase goods and services preferably from a given source of supply.

THE BUYING RESPONSES

Organization buying is not a single act but a process that includes a complex set of activities and conditions which induce complex response actions. This fact suggests that one should be concerned with a variety of buying responses and not merely with one single response. What are these responses, and how are they related to the supplier's objectives?

Purchase—or, from the marketing man's point of view, making a sale—is commonly stated as the prime marketing objective. But when one examines organizational buying behavior, one must recognize that purchase is only one of a possible set of responses an organizational buying center can make. Searching for further information, engaging in a negotiation process, expressing attitudes toward and preference for a particular source of supply are also responses that should be of considerable importance to the supplying organization.

An acceptable model of a buying decision process should suggest, therefore, that each of the decision stages, while a necessary stage for the next one (in a "hierarchy-of-effects" model [4]), may also be a dependent variable

[4] The concept of "hierarchy of effects" was developed originally to explain consumers' movement through various decision stages from unawareness to purchase. Since no one really knows what are the decision processes a consumer goes through, an alternative concept of "correlates of effects" was developed. Cf. Homer M. Dalbey, Irwin Gross, and Yoram Wind, *Advertising Measurement and Decision Making* (Boston: Allyn & Bacon, Inc., 1968).

in its own right and can be viewed as a legitimate response of the buying center.

Provided that a buying decision process is identified, and provided that one accepts the concept of a "hierarachy of effects," the objectives of the organizational marketer are to coordinate the buying roles and to move the buying center through the decision process to the conclusive act of selecting a supplier while at the same time developing and cultivating a mutually beneficial long-run relationship with the buying organization.

In attempting to achieve this goal, the marketer can use as guidelines and measures of his success the various communication and purchase responses of the buying organization. The purchase responses include not just whether or not a purchase was made (a need for a product may result in a "make" rather than a "buy" decision) but also the buying organization's responses over time—i.e., the brand and source loyalty patterns.

The communication responses include both verbal and nonverbal as well as "real life" and "research bound" responses. Table 3–2 presents the four

TABLE 3–2. Classification of Communication Responses

| | | Nature of Response | |
		Verbal	Action (Nonverbal)
Context of Assessing the Response	"Real Life"	Word of Mouth Communication Attitudes	Search for Information Request for Bid Evaluation of Information Negotiation and Bargaining
	"Research Bound"	Awareness Attitude	Perceptions of and Preferences among Suppliers

possible types of nonpurchase responses. The context of assessing the responses can be either a "real life" situation—in which the marketing personnel can assess the buying organization's responses in the normal course of conducting their tasks—or a research bound response generated in the course of a study of the buying process. In either case the responses can be verbal or nonverbal. Given the bias of most verbal responses, the development of nonmetric, multidimensional scaling techniques has generated considerable interest as a measurement of nonverbal consumer responses. These measures, primarily of the subject's perceptions of and preferences among a set of stimuli (suppliers, products, ads, etc.), are also applicable to the study of organizational buying behavior, and should be considered as another possible measure of the response of the buying organization.[5]

[5] For an application of multidimensional scaling techniques to industrial marketing, see Yoram Wind, "Mathematical Analysis of Perception and Preference for Industrial Marketing," in Keith Cox and Ben M. Enis, eds., A New Measure of Responsibility for Marketing (Chicago: American Marketing Association Proceedings No. 27, June 1968), 284–94.

Since the objective of the suppliers is the establishment of mutually beneficial long-run relationships with the buying organization, the relevant measures have to be capable of portraying the buying response not only at a point in time but also over time. All of the communication measures satisfy this requirement because they can be measured over time and changes in their nature and magnitude can be traced.

The "So What" Question

Having developed a model of organizational buying behavior, the question still is "so what?"—what are the advantages of having such a model? In exploring the nature of our model and its idiosyncratic characteristics, it might be useful to compare it first with existing consumer behavior models. In this respect the major difference is that, in contrast to the existing consumer behavior models, this model does not claim to know what is the exact buying decision-making process. Instead, recognizing the situation-dependent and dynamic nature of buying behavior, it presents the major sets of variables (blocks) that marketing personnel should identify in their attempt to understand buying behavior. Furthermore, it deals explicitly with organizational buying behavior.

Recognizing that no deterministic model of organizational buying behavior can be developed, the purpose of developing the model is threefold:

1. To identify the major sets of variables affecting the organizational buying decisions;
2. To highlight the current state of knowledge with respect to the various relationships among the key variables in the buying system;
3. To provide guidelines for future research in the area of organizational buying behavior.

The next four chapters seek to achieve the first two objectives of the model. An initial attempt at suggesting some areas which have not yet been studied and which may prove useful in improving our understanding and ability to predict organizational buying behavior are suggested in the final chapter.

4

ENVIRONMENTAL INFLUENCES ON ORGANIZATIONAL BUYING BEHAVIOR

The organizational buying decision process is significantly influenced by the relationships of the organization and its members with the larger environment. The complex nature of environmental influence reflects the interaction of those physical, technological, economic, political, legal, and cultural factors and institutions that comprise the environment. These relationships obviously become especially complex as the organization extends its concerns beyond national boundaries so that all of these environmental factors take on values specific to a particular country. Given the broad scope of environmental factors, the purpose of this chapter is simply to suggest the major dimensions of environmental influence on organizational buying decisions. In addition to this broad overview, however, we shall also consider in somewhat greater detail the changing nature of the environment and four aspects of environmental influence of special significance for organizational buying:

1. ecological consequences of buying decisions;
2. technological forecasting;
3. professions as subcultures;
4. the diffusion of innovations.

Nature of Environmental Influence

Environmental influences are subtle and pervasive. They are hard to identify and describe, and they provide the context within which organizational, interpersonal, and individual factors in turn exert their influence. One way of conceptualizing environmental factors is as a set of constraints on the organization—a set of predetermined boundaries beyond the control of the organization and its members. In another sense, the environment is a source of information which the organizational buyer takes into account in his decision-making behavior. This reckoning may be *explicit,* as is the case when one considers the significance of anti-trust regulation for a given decision, or it may be *implicit,* as is the case with basic cultural values and political beliefs.

It is useful to make further distinctions between the kinds of environmental influences and the institutions that exert those influences. The foregoing comments have identified six kinds of environmental influences: physical, technological, economic, political, legal, and cultural. These influences may be exerted through a variety of institutional forms, including business firms (suppliers, customers, and competitors being three major subclasses), governments, labor unions, trade associations, professional groups, religious organizations, educational and medical institutions, and political parties. The types and functioning of such institutional forms vary significantly from country to country and provide one of the most important bases for distinguishing one country from another.

The six sets of environmental influences are highly interrelated, are subject to continuous forces of change, and are of both direct and indirect relevance to the organizational buying task. Similarly, the institutions which operate in the organizational environment are also interlinked, dynamic in nature, and divisible into task and nontask categories. The suppliers, labor unions, government, competitors, customers, trade associations, and professional groups have in some cases direct task relevance; at other times, however, their effect on the organizational decisions is at best indirect and similar to the effect of educational, religious, and other social institutions. A simple visual model of the influence on organizational buying decisions of each of the six sets of environmental factors as exerted through a variety of institutional forms is presented in Figure 4–1. As can be seen in this figure, environmental factors influence the buying decision process in four rather distinct ways. First, they define the availability of goods and services to the buying organization. Second, they define the general business conditions within which the firm must operate, including the business cycle, the political climate, the legal environment, and the availability of monetary resources. Third, they define the values and norms (for the society as a whole and for subgroups within that society) that provide an important set of criteria against which to evaluate alternative buying actions. Finally, the environment provides a flow of information to the buying organization and its members concerning both task and nontask communication on the availability of goods and services, general business conditions, and values and norms. Especially important as an information source are marketing stimuli provided by suppliers. Although the primary contact of the buyers is with the various suppliers, any organizational buying requires some contact with other organizations as well. The relationships of the organizational members with their environment are, therefore, not only bargaining relationships, but also competitive (that is, the consequences of competitive actions), cooperative (with suppliers, clients, etc.), and of a coalition formation nature.[1]

[1] J. D. Thompson and W. J. McEwan, "Organization Goals and Environment," *American Sociological Review,* XXIII (February, 1958), 23–31.

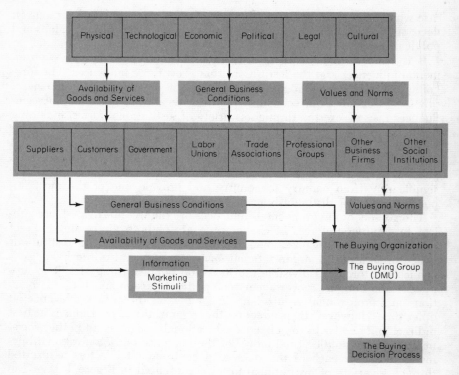

FIGURE 4–1. A Model of Environmental Effects on the Organizational Buying Process

In the following pages we will consider more specifically the nature of each set of environmental influences and the various institutions that exert those influences on the organizational buying process.

Kinds of Environmental Influences

PHYSICAL

At the most basic level, the physical environment affects the behavior of organizational members and defines the constraints within which the buying task must be accomplished and the options available to the buying organization. Such physical factors as the climate and the geographic location of the organization define the avaliability of products of forest, farm, and mine and create the demand for certain goods and services such as heating fuel and transportation. The desire to be near certain raw materials, or a pool of labor, or transportation often dictates the final selection of location for an organization.

Furthermore, the geographical location of a supplier may have an im-

portant bearing on whether he will be selected or not. This is especially so when the buying organization has a policy of preference for local suppliers and when the nature of the buying task requires close interpersonal communication and service.

Another aspect of the physical environment that places constraints on the buying organization is the plant and equipment with which it is operating at any given moment. Of course, one kind of buying decision involves the replacement of plant and equipment and that obviously changes the constraints. For many other buying decisions, however, consideration must be given to existing facilities as these define buying requirements.

Ecological Consequences of Buying Decisions. A new and growing awareness of the impact of economic activity on the physical environment is fast becoming a major consideration in organizational buying decisions. This new concern is forcing a broader definition of the buying task to include consequences on the physical environment. The relentless pressure of economic activity on the environment, especially in the United States (which has 6 percent of the world's population but consumes 40 percent of its resources), has taken its toll to the point where concern for the environment must assume top priority in many kinds of buying decisions. New regulations at the local, state, and federal levels are forcing many manufacturers to install equipment for water purification and air pollution control.

Pressure for more careful consideration of the ecological consequences of buying decisions has come from many quarters, including all levels of government and private groups concerned with conservation and political action. This new concern for the physical environment will undoubtedly change the constraints within which organizational buying decisions must be made.

TECHNOLOGICAL

The technological environment is in a sense the part of the physical environment that has been created by man. It includes such broad realms of human activity as communication and transportation systems as well as electronic data processing capabilities, biological and medical knowledge and practice, metals technologies, and energy conversion techniques. In general terms, technology defines the availability of goods and services to the buying organization and defines the horizon for the quality and level of services to be offered by the buying organization to the clientele it serves.

In addition to influencing the determination of what is bought, technology also influences the nature of the buying process. The buying process in many formal organizations has undergone rather fundamental changes resulting from the use of the computer, which has made possible automatic reordering and inventory control for routinely purchased consumable items and has permitted much more careful analysis of complex buying decisions involving substantial financial commitments. Improved purchasing technology has led to better buying decisions.

Technological Forecasting. In many kinds of purchasing, the ability to forecast future technological developments becomes important in making the final decision. Technological forecasting can help to predict and define long-term buying tasks. Virtually all equipment purchases involve some calculated judgment about the likelihood that present technology will be made obsolete.

Several techniques have been developed for technological forecasting. Among the most common technological forecasting techniques are: casual forecasts, extrapolations, objectives networks and relevancy trees, the "Delphi" Technique, scenario development, and socio-politico-economic modeling.[2]

Technological forecasting, especially in an input-output context that considers technological interdependence among industry sectors, can help to identify changes in demand for particular goods and services. Such analyses can help the organization avoid, or at least plan for, critical shortages of key raw materials and resulting high prices. Technological forecasting can also suggest the time period within which major changes in a given technology are likely to occur. Specific consideration of the technological environment within which the organization will be operating in the future can be a significant aid in planning long-run buying activities.

ECONOMIC

The economic environment for the buying organization reflects a wide variety of factors and has both task and nontask consequences. Among the most important elements of the economic environment are price and wage conditions, the availability of money and credit, the strength of demand in the consumer sector, and inventory levels in key industry sectors.

The general economic setting of any country is reflected in the country's level of employment, its price stability, its economic growth, and its balance of payments situation. These factors determine not only the general economic setting under which any organization operates, but also the nature of the activities of the other institutions which are members of the socioeconomic system—activities which in turn may also affect the organization's buying decisions.

Although most of the effects of the economic setting can be considered to be not directly task-related, some of them may have direct impact on the buying task. Where products have market prices established by fluctuations in supply and demand, the buying task may be defined in terms of anticipating price levels at various points in time. Similarly, expectations

---

[2] These six techniques are described in somewhat greater detail in A. P. Lien, P. Anton, and J. W. Duncan, *Technological Forecasting: Tools, Techniques, and Applications,* A.M.A. Bulletin No. 115 (New York: American Management Association, 1968).

of work stoppages in key industries may cause buying organizations to buy ahead and stockpile important materials; in addition, the availability of credit or other methods of financing transactions may be important factors in defining the buying task.

Nontask effects of the economic environment sometimes are reflected in the general optimism or pessimism of professional buyers, which in turn influences their buying behavior.

The economic environment has its greatest impact in defining the availability of goods and services, the ability of buying organizations to finance the transactions, and the prices that will be paid. Careful forecasting of general economic conditions as well as more specific economic variables, such as the prices of key commodities, can therefore be a significant aid in long-range planning of the buying task.

POLITICAL

The political environment is defined here to include governmental activities as well as relationships among governments at various level and the activities of political parties. More specifically, political influences include tariff and trade agreements among nations, lobbying activities with state and federal governments, military spending, government funding of certain kinds of buying activities, and administrative attitudes toward various business and social activities and priorities.

LEGAL

Governments also exert a more direct influence through the creation of a legal environment within which buying activities must take place. Government regulation may operate to determine specifications for what is bought as well as the terms of sale. Influence may be exerted to protect competition in both buying and selling industries and to maintain standards of quality for products and services.

CULTURAL

Culture is defined as the integral whole consisting of the emerging pattern of all material and behavioral arrangements that have been learned and shared by people as members of society and accepted by them as means of defining and solving problems. Stated differently, culture is the sum of shared meanings that characterizes a society. Culture provides values— i.e., those shared ideals that arouse positive or negative emotional and behavioral responses from the members of society toward specific objects in the environment. Values influence both the organization and its members. Culture as reflected in values, mores, customs, habits, norms, traditions, and so on will influence the structure and functioning of the organization and the way the members of the organization feel and act toward one another and toward various aspects of the environment.

Both the culture and its subcultures effect organizational buying behavior primarily by determining the values both of all those participating in the buying process and of the organization itself.

The values held by organizational members are also important determinants of the organizational values, which must be both socially accepted as legitimate values (that is, congruent with the values of the given society) and essential to the operation, preservation, and enhancement of the organization itself.

Professions as Subcultures.   In many instances professional people provide a form of subculture within the organizational buying process. Members of a subculture share values, norms, artifacts, behavior patterns, language, and so forth, with each subculture tending to be distinctive in these areas. Professional employees within organizations often feel strong allegiance to their professions. Professional associations such as the American Medical Association or the National Association of Purchasing Management can also be significant influences on organizational buying.

Such subcultural influences can be very important in the organizational buying process and the marketer should make every effort to understand these influences and to adjust his marketing strategy to them.

To summarize, the organizational buying process is influenced by the physical, technological, economic, political, legal, and cultural environment in which the firm and its members are operating. The marketing strategist must carefully appraise how each set of factors will shape the buying decision process and determine the values and attitudes of key decision influencers.

Institutional Forms

Environmental influences are exerted on the organization primarily through a variety of social institutions. The operation of such institutions has been briefly suggested in the preceding remarks but now we must look more closely at the functioning of some of the most important institutions shaping the environment within which the organization operates.

SUPPLIERS

Companies that are potential suppliers to the buying organization are certainly one of the most important institutions in the buying environment. These potential suppliers define the technology that is available to the buyer and the conditions under which it is offered for sale. Through their own promotional and distribution efforts, and through arrangements with various middlemen, potential suppliers must perform several important functions prior to making the sale, including providing an assortment of merchandise, storing the product in convenient locations, transporting the product, contacting potential customers, negotiating the terms of the transaction, financing the transaction, and providing follow-up services. The bundle of services surrounding the product may actually be more important than the physical product itself in defining the best solution to the buying organization's problems. Perhaps the major contribution of suppliers to the buying environment, however, is through the quality of information which they provide through channels that have the highest probability of being useful to the potential customers. Such information must be consistent with the values and norms of the larger society in terms of both message content and method of delivery.

CUSTOMERS

In the most general sense, virtually all organizations exist to serve some clientele or "customer" group, so that their buying decisions usually will have some influence, direct or indirect, on the quality of service offered to that clientele. When customers are other organizations, the goals and procedures of those organizations provide criteria that can determine the wisdom of a proposed buying alternative. Important considerations for any organization's buying decisions are, therefore, how acceptable the action will be with its own customers and clientele, and what its impact will be on firm-client relations.

GOVERNMENT

Government is an important institution affecting organizational buying in five distinct and highly significant task- and nontask-related roles. First, the government is a regulator defining the legal environment within which buying decisions must be made and constraining the courses of action available to both buyers and sellers. Second, the government is an important economic factor influencing the availability of money, the level of consumer demand, and wage and price conditions in certain sectors of the economy. Third, the government, through its spending for research and development (which in the aggregate exceeds spending for research and development in the private sector of the economy), significantly influences the technological environment within which the buying organization is operating. Fourth, as a political entity the government influences national goals and priorities, trade relationships with other countries, the level of military spending, policies toward private industry, and spending for various kinds of private and quasi-public purposes such as aid to small business and public health. In these sales the government is also a manipulator and distributor of economic rewards which may change the buyer's cost and value balance with respect to specific situations and suppliers. Finally, government is an important customer for many suppliers.

As a customer, government is unique in that it simultaneously defines both what is needed (like any other customer) and the environment within which the transaction will occur. It can determine the conditions under which products will be bought, who is eligible to be considered as a supplier, the terms of sale, the penalties for nonperformance of contract terms, and so on. Although this power of the government to define the buying environment is especially true at the federal level, and even more specifically for national defense spending (where Armed Services Procurement Regulations define in detail the conditions of buying and even the profit that will be allowed to suppliers under stated conditions), it is true to some extent for virtually all government levels where the power to regulate exists along with the power to purchase.

LABOR UNIONS

Labor unions influence the organizational buying environment through their impact on both buyers and sellers. In buying organizations, labor union influence is felt in two respects. First, unions may significantly influence the specifications for what is to be bought in situations where it is felt that the welfare of union members is influenced by the buying decision. Second, unions may influence the alternative sources of supply available to buying organizations by requirements that certain suppliers be avoided or that others be favored, usually as tactics to influence union relationships with these potential suppliers.

Union influence on selling organizations is through the collective bargaining process that determines wages and therefore the cost structure of the supplier, and through the threat of work stoppages in order to achieve union objectives. A seller's ability to compete will be seriously impaired if he is unable to assure potential customers of a reliable source of supply.

TRADE ASSOCIATIONS AND PROFESSIONAL ORGANIZATIONS

Trade associations are typically combinations of firms in a given industry and usually have as their purpose the sharing of information on industry activity. Other typical areas of cooperative activity through trade associations include lobbying with government officials, public relations activities, and industry education functions. In certain instances, trade associations may help industry members evaluate new products or may facilitate the exchange of information between industry members and potential suppliers.

These associations often have journals that provide one source of information about new products and services to their members. More importantly, they may provide members with standards of behavior that must be very carefully understood by those who wish to sell to these professions. The professional values of purchasing managers, for example, have been codified into standards that are communicated to members of the National Association of Purchasing Management.

The professional person considering alternative buying actions for his organization may give top priority to those criteria, which he assumes would be used by other members of his profession. He will use his profession as a reference group for standards for his own behavior and will make judgments about the consistency of alternative actions with professional values and standards. The professional subculture exerts its influence through professional associations that provide a flow of information among members and help them codify and enforce standards of professional conduct.

OTHER BUSINESS FIRMS

In addition to the firms' suppliers, customers, and competitors, other business firms which are not directly related to the buying task may have some indirect effect on a firm's buying activities.

SOCIAL INSTITUTIONS

The members of any buying organization are all members of a variety of social, religious, educational, and recreational institutions in which they perform various roles. Possible role conflict between an individual's role in any of these institutions and his buying roles may have substantial effect on the organizational buying activities. Furthermore, the organization as a whole has certain nontask responsibilities and links with a variety of social institutions, such as foundations, charities, and other civic institutions, which may affect indirectly the buying policies and activities of the organization.

The Changing Environment

The Year 2000: A Framework for Speculation on the Next Thirty Three Years; The Future of the Future; An Alternative Future for America; Mankind 2000; Environment and Policy: The Next Fifty Years; Environment and Change: The Next Fifty Years; and *The 21st Century* [3] are all titles of books dealing explicitly with the changing environment. The proliferation of such studies and speculations and the establishment of scientific societies for the study of the future, such as the "World Future Society: An Association for the Study of Alternative Futures," with a regular professional publication, are all indicators of the growing recognition of

[3] Herman Kahn and Anthony J. Wiener, *The Year 2000* (New York: The Macmillan Company, 1967); John McHale, *The Future of the Future* (New York: George Braziller, 1969); Robert Theobald (ed.), *An Alternative Future for America* (Chicago: Swallow Press, 1968); Robert Jungk and Johan Galtung, eds., *Mankind 2000* (Oslo: Universitets-forlaget, 1968); William R. Ewald, Jr., ed., *Environment and Policy: The Next Fifty Years* (Bloomington: Indiana University Press, 1968); ———, *Environment and Change: The Next Fifty Years* (Bloomington: Indiana University Press, 1968); and Fred Warshofsky, *The 21st Century: The New Age of Exploration* (New York: Viking Press, 1969).

the dynamic nature of the environment and the importance of taking explicit account of changes in it.

A systematic effort to forecast these environmental changes can aid planning. Although environmental forecasting is currently much less developed than technological forecasting, these forecasts cannot be limited to technological forecasting alone and should be directed at forecasting the whole environmental system.

The Diffusion of Innovations.   One expression of the dynamic nature of society is the emphasis on the diffusion process, which is the process by which an innovation spreads through a social system over time. There are marked differences among industries, professions, and other "social systems" of organizational buyers in the speed with which they adopt new products and services (and new management practices and other innovations as well). Individual organizations also vary markedly in the speed with which they adopt new products, depending upon such factors as the degree of centralization of buying responsibility, the number of people involved in the buying decision, the size of the organization, the nature of the information channels operating within the organization, and the ability of the organization to finance the innovation. Those organizations that are among the first to adopt an innovation are likely to be those for whom the innovation offers the greatest benefits and advantage over competing organizations and those that can tolerate the risk of innovation, both in financial terms and in terms of the possible negative consequences from unsatisfactory performance of the innovation. Finally, innovative organizations are likely to grow faster and to be more "aggressive" in expanding the scope of their operations.[4]

Diffusion is a social influence process. The actions of one buying organization exert an influence on other organizations, either through providing information or through creating pressure on these other organizations to change their behavior. Those that adopt an innovation first make the innovation visible to the others and are in a position to provide information about it. If the innovating organization gains some advantage over its competitors through the adoption of the innovation—as when airlines first adopted jet aircraft, for example—then the innovator also creates pressures for others to adopt the innovation. Those who adopt first take on greater risks than those who adopt later because these later organizations have less uncertainty about the performance of the innovation.

A recent study has failed to find any evidence of widespread word-of-mouth activity among industrial firms in the adoption of new products. Other using companies were not regarded as important sources of information about new products and services. It was found, however, that later adopters did find it helpful to observe or otherwise learn about the experiences of earlier adopters with new products, but that the salesman typically was the intermediary for such information. In other words, the

4 Frederick E. Webster, Jr., "New Product Adoption in Industrial Markets: A Framework for Analysis," *Journal of Marketing*, XXXIII (July 1969), 35–39.

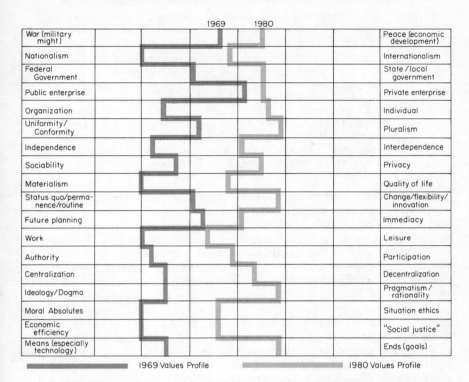

	1969	1980	
War (military might)			Peace (economic development)
Nationalism			Internationalism
Federal Government			State/local government
Public enterprise			Private enterprise
Organization			Individual
Uniformity/ Conformity			Pluralism
Independence			Interdependence
Sociability			Privacy
Materialism			Quality of life
Status quo/perma- nence/routine			Change/flexibility/ innovation
Future planning			Immediacy
Work			Leisure
Authority			Participation
Centralization			Decentralization
Ideology/Dogma			Pragmatism/ rationality
Moral Absolutes			Situation ethics
Economic efficiency			"Social justice"
Means (especially technology)			Ends (goals)

1969 Values Profile   1980 Values Profile

FIGURE 4–2.   Profile of Significant Value-System Changes: 1969–1980 as Seen by General Electric's Business Environment Section

Reproduced, with permission, from Ian H. Wilson, "How Our Values Are Changing," The Futurist: A Journal of Forecasts, Trends, and Ideas About the Future, IV (February, 1970), 5–9, published by the World Future Society, P.O. Box 19285, 20th St. Station, Washington, D.C. 20036.

salesman for the company marketing the innovation finds it helpful to talk about or demonstrate successful applications in other companies.[5]

Summary

Environmental influences on the organizational buying process come from many institutions within society and can be classified into six categories: physical, technological, economic, political, legal, and cultural. These factors can affect organizational buying behavior in two ways:

1. The environmental factors can be perceived, reacted to, and taken into account by the organizational members in

[5] Frederick E. Webster, Jr., "Informal Communication in Industrial Markets," *Journal of Marketing Research*, VII (May 1970), 186–89.

making their buying decisions. In this context the environmental factors affect the decision-makers' values and preferences, choices and actions.

2. The environmental factors may be conceived of as constraints on the execution of strategies designed to achieve
the envisaged buying goals. Such limitations on performance and outcomes do not depend on the decision-making
unit's perception of the environment—that is to say, being
ignorant of certain elements of the environment or not taking them into account in reaching a decision does not pre-
vent these environmental factors from affecting, sometimes
in a decisive way, the operational outcome of the buying
decisions.[6]

A satisfactory performance of the organizational buying process obviously requires that the organizational members attempt to minimize the
second type of environmental effect. Therefore, in focusing on the first
type of effect we have distinguished between four major ways in which the
environment affects the organizational buying process—by defining the
availability of goods and services, by determining general business conditions, by affecting the values of the organizational members, and finally
by providing information to the buying organization and its members.

The environmental factors are likely to vary significantly from one
country to another and the ability of selling firms to understand these basic
differences is undoubtedly a major determinant of their ability to compete
at the multinational level. Although these influences are basic, they are also
hard to identify and measure because they are so intimately woven into
the fabric of the environment. Nonetheless, marketing strategies aimed at
organizational buyers must be sensitive to these very important environmental influences because they define the boundaries within which the
buyer-seller relationship must be developed.

[6] For an elaboration of these two environmental effects see Harold and
Margaret Sprout, *The Ecological Perspective on Human Affairs* (Princeton, N.J.:
Princeton University Press, 1965).

5

ORGANIZATIONAL INFLUENCES ON BUYING BEHAVIOR

Organizational buying behavior takes place in the context of a formal organization. It is motivated by the purposes of the organization and constrained by the organization's financial, technological, and human resources. The purpose of this chapter is to define the organizational variables that influence organizational buying behavior and to review theories and research findings from the study of organizations that can help our understanding of the organizational buying decision process.

Nature and Scope of Organizational Variables

According to a view proposed by Leavitt, organizations are multi-variate systems composed of four sets of interacting variables:

tasks—the work to be performed in accomplishing the objectives of the organization;

structure—systems of communication, authority, status, rewards, and work flow;

technology—problem-solving inventions used by the firm, including plant and equipment and programs for organizing and managing work;

people—the actors in the system.

These four interacting sets of variables are highly dependent on one another and define the information, expectations, goals, attitudes, and assumptions used by each of the individual actors in his decision-making activities. Figure 5–1 is a schematic presentation of the influence of these four sets of variables in the organizational buying process.[1]

[1] Harold J. Leavitt, "Applied Organization Change in Industry: Structural, Technical, and Human Approaches," in William W. Cooper, Harold J. Leavitt, and Maynard W. Shelly, II, *New Perspectives in Organization Research* (New York: John Wiley & Sons, Inc., 1964), 55–71.

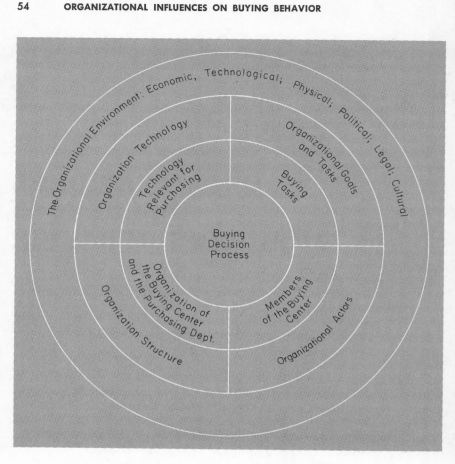

FIGURE 5–1. A Model of the Buying Organization

    Implicit in the model of the buying organization presented in Figure 5–1 are several assertions. First, the model implies that each of the four elements of the buying organization (people, technology, structure, and tasks) is best viewed as a subset of each of these four sets of variables in the larger organization. The logical corollary of this view, which stresses the interdependency of buying with other parts of the organization, is that understanding the buying organization requires understanding the larger organizational system of interdependent elements. Second, the model stresses the interdependency between the organization and its larger environment; this interdependency was carefully examined in the previous chapter. The third important feature of this model is that each of the four subsystems of organizational variables interacts with and influences each of the others. The people influence the structure, technology, and tasks; technology influences people, structure, and tasks; and so on. Finally, the model defines four specific and distinct aspects of the organizational buying process that must be analyzed by the marketing strategist, each of which must be carefully considered in the development of the marketing strategy designed to influence that process.

BUYING TASKS

The buying task is just one of many tasks performed by the organization in pursuit of its objectives, and the purpose of all organizational buying is to help the organization achieve its objectives. The solution of that specific problem then becomes the goal for the buying process. The work of buying must then be broken down into tasks which can be classified in many different ways, such as according to purpose, amount of expenditure involved, or type of goods or services being purchased. The primary functions that motivate buying decisions and the major kinds of buying tasks will reflect the basic nature and purpose of the organization. A retailer's characteristic or typical buying task is quite different from that of a manufacturer and they both differ from that of a hospital, although all three will also have certain buying tasks in common.

One generally useful way of classifying buying tasks is to make a distinction among several stages in the buying decision process, treating each as a separate task. Other important distinctions that help define buying tasks include: (a) whether the buying decision is routine ("programmed") or requires managerial attention at all decision stages; (b) whether demand for the product is generated within the organization or by forces outside the organization; and (c) whether the responsibility for purchasing in the organization is centralized or decentralized.

Because buying tasks are defined by organizational objectives and because the buying center may be composed of individual actors with responsibilities for different subsets of objectives, there is likely to be conflict among definitions of buying tasks within the buying center. Thus, even to the extent that the formal organization provides policies and procedures for the direction of the buying decision, as part of its "programming" technology, the final resolution of buying tasks is certain to be considerably influenced by interpersonal factors within the context of the formal organization.

BUYING STRUCTURE

The structure of the organization has five systems that influence the nature of the buying process: communication, authority, status, rewards, and work flow.

Communication. The communication system has five interacting elements—sources, messages, media, receivers, and responses. These elements are summarized in a simple definition of the process of communication as *"who* says *what* in which *channel* to *whom* with what *result."* Within an organization, communication performs four essential functions.[2]

1. The *information functions.* Organizational actors depend upon a flow of timely and accurate information for the performance of their duties; they are likewise responsible for generating a flow of timely and accurate information to other members of the organization. One very useful way of analyzing organizations is to specify for each position the inputs and outputs of information required for functioning of the organization. The performance of the organizational actors is heavily influenced by the quality of information available to them.

2. The *command* and *instructive* functions. Organizational members who are hierarchically superior to others issue a variety of commands, instructions, orders, directives, procedures, and so on that have the function of ordering and instructing subordinates concerning the performance of their responsibilities. These messages have the effect of constraining the individual actors' freedom to exercise their own judgment as well as creating expectations about evaluation and the distribution of organizational rewards.

3. The *influence* and *persuasive* functions. Organizational members transmit messages which have the purpose of altering the attitudes and behavior of other organizational members. These functions may be performed by any members of the organization with respect to any other members, and do not depend upon the authority and reporting structure of the organization. The purpose of such messages may be either to influence the members' behavior directly or to influence the frame of reference (predispositions or attitudes) within which members interpret information from other parts of the organization or from outside the organization.

4. The *integrative* functions. Some messages have the purpose of strengthening, altering, or facilitating the functioning of the organization itself. One author defines these functions as ". . . all behavioral operations which: (1) serve to keep the system in operation; (2) serve to regulate the interactional process; (3) cross reference particular messages to comprehensibility in a particular context, and (4) relate the particular context to the larger context of which the particular interaction is but a special situation." [3]

---

[2] The following comments draw heavily upon Lee Thayer, *Communication and Communication Systems* (Homewood, Ill.: Richard D. Irwin, Inc., 1968), 187–250.

[3] Ray Birdwhistell, as quoted in T. A. Sebeok, A. S. Hayes, and Mary C. Bateson, eds., *Approaches to Semiotics* (The Hague: Mouton, 1964), 161–62.

Each of these four functions of the communication system is important in understanding the functioning of the organization as it influences the nature of the organizational buying process. Members of the buying center must be informed as to the nature of the buying problem, the criteria that should be used in evaluating alternative suppliers, and the availability of alternative sources of supply. Reference to the five stages of the buying decision process in Figure 3-2 (page 31) immediately suggests the importance of complete and accurate information at each stage of the decision process. The performance of an individual member of the buying center will reflect the quality of the information available to him. The marketing communicator must make sure that accurate and complete information is available to *all* members of the buying center.

The command and instructive functions of information affect the buying center by defining the discretion and latitude of individuals in influencing the buying decision. It is essential that the marketer understand clearly the kinds of commands and instructions that have been issued within the buying organization to influence and constrain the various members of the buying center.

Influence and persuasive functions are performed by all members of the organization and provide the substance of interpersonal interaction within the organizational context. The nature of these influence processes will be examined much more carefully in Chapter 6; here it is important to note, however, that in their attempts to direct subordinates, persons in positions of authority actually may rely more upon their ability to influence and persuade than upon their authority to issue commands and instructions. The nature of the formal organization itself can help or impede such influence attempts.

The integrative function of communication is essential in assuring smooth and coordinated operation of the buying center. Because the buying center is an *ad hoc* creation, peculiar to each buying situation, the problem of coordinating and directing the interaction of its members may be a serious one. This coordination function is one of the primary roles of the manager of purchasing, although the task of ensuring that all members of the buying center are operating with consistent sets of goals, expectations, and information may also fall to the vendor's salesman.

In summary, the communication system within the organization influences the behavior of members of the buying center by performing the functions of informing, commanding and instructing, persuading and influencing, and integrating the performance of individual actors. It is important to remember that these functions are not performed in isolation, however, but in interaction with the other organizational structure systems of authority, work flow, status, and rewards, as well as with the other systems of technology, tasks, and people. Nonetheless, the communication subsystem can be isolated for purposes of analysis and it will usually be helpful to the marketing strategist to so isolate it.

Authority. The authority structure is one of the primary features of an organization. Authority can be thought of as the power to judge, command, or otherwise act so as to influence the behavior of others. Dornbusch, Scott, Busing, and Laing have proposed a distinction among four systems of authority rights. *Allocation* rights give actor A the right to communicate to actor B an organizational goal that B is expected to pursue. *Criteria* rights give A the right to establish the criteria by which B's performance is to be evaluated. *Sampling* rights give A the right to examine some or all of B's performance and to communicate this to one or more of those who evaluate B's performance. *Evaluation* rights give A the right to assess B's performance and to distribute rewards or punishments based upon that evaluation.[4] To these four kinds of rights, Knight has added a fifth: *authority reversal* rights, which give actor A some subset of the above four rights over B in specified situations while giving B a similar subset of rights over A in other specified situations.[5] The addition of the authority reversal right to this classification has the merit of recognizing that the distribution of authority may not be consistent over all buying situations, but instead may vary to reflect the specific nature of the buying task and the composition of the buying center. Furthermore, it suggests that an arrangement of authority rights may come about by mutual consent among the organizational members without specific provision in the formal organization itself.

No factor is more critical for an understanding of the buying process than the distribution of authority and responsibility within the buying center. One operational way of defining and understanding the authority system is by the use of a Linear Responsibility Chart which specifies the various relationships that may exist between any member of the buying center and any buying-related function and work with which he may be associated as policy-maker, supervisor, coordinator, doer, or influencer.[6]

The formal aspect of the authority system will be reflected primarily in the degree of centralization of the buying decision. Because the question of centralization also involves other aspects of the formal organization, as well as authority structures, it will be treated separately later on in this chapter.

Status.   A status is a position in a hierarchy with respect to other individuals. Any organization has two status systems—the formal status system and the informal (social) status system, which are related to each other in such a way that the position of an organizational member in one system is not always a good predictor of his status in the other system. Every status has associated with it certain specified duties and privileges with respect to other members of the organization. A *role* is the performance of those duties and privileges by the person who occupies that status. A status

[4] S. M. Dornbusch, W. R. Scott, B. C. Busing, and J. D. Laing, "Evaluation Processes and Authority Structures," paper presented at the 1965 meeting of the American Sociological Association.

[5] Kenneth E. Knight, "Behavioral Sciences and the Design of Research and Development Organizations," Working Paper No. 72, Graduate School of Business, Stanford University, 1964.

[6] Alfred G. Larke, "Linear Responsibility Chart—New Tool for Executive Control," *Dun's Review and Modern Industry*, LXIV (August, 1954), 46–50.

takes on meaning by its relationship to other statuses while a role takes on meaning through being performed. The concept of status and the concept of role are inseparable.[7] Positions within the informal status system are important in determining the quality of (informal) interpersonal interaction within the organization and a discussion of these influences is, once again, postponed until the next chapter.

Status within the formal organization is defined by the assignment of the individual to a position in the hierarchy by his superior and through the specific provisions of the job description for that position. Status in the hierarchy will be a major factor determining the authority rights of the individual and the nature of the communication and work flow that will occupy his attention. Specifically in the case of the buying decision, status in the organization may define the stage in the buying process at which the individual becomes involved, as well as the number of stages that will come within the authority of the actor. Persons higher up in the hierarchy will have a wider range of discretion and will be involved (or have more authority to become involved when they so desire) in more stages of the buying process.

Professional purchasing managers with a serious interest in expanding the scope of their authority within the buying organization in order to perform more functions in the buying process may strive to obtain positions higher in the hierarchy. Redefining the purchasing function as "Materials Management" or "Logistics" is often part of a strategy aimed at redefining the organization structure so as to give the buying executive maximum status (and authority) within the organization by permitting him to assume the title of vice president reporting directly to the president.

Rewards. Individuals become members of formal organizations in anticipation of the rewards given by the organization. Rewards may be both financial and nonfinancial and the distribution of them always depends upon some form of evaluation system involving judgments by other organizational actors about the contribution of the individual's performance to the accomplishment of organizational objectives. The reward system as part of the organization structure is therefore intimately entwined with the communication, authority, and status subsystems of organization structure, as well as with the broader systems of goals and tasks, technology, and people. The individual's performance will in turn reflect his perception of each of these other elements of the organization as they influence the determination of his rewards. The behavior of individual members of the buying center can often be best explained by their perceptions of the distribution of rewards and how each of these other organizational systems influences that distribution, rather than by reference to the deceptively objective statements of job descriptions or other trappings of the formal organization. The individual's subjective perception concerning the distribution of rewards may reflect information received from others in the organization as well as his interpretation of previous experience in terms

[7] George C. Homans, *The Human Group* (New York: Harcourt Brace Jovanovich, Inc., 1950), 11.

of what kinds of actions were rewarded. It will also reflect the individual's needs. Rewards of affection and (informal or formal) status may be more important than financial rewards.

A careful analysis of the reward structure of the organization as it affects the individual therefore can be a most significant factor in making predictions of the response to marketing effort by members of the buying center. The starting point for such an analysis must be the individual's needs and wants, his goals and aspirations, for these determine the value of alternative kinds of rewards to him. Then the analyst can consider how other organizational variables interact to determine the rewards available to the individual actors and their perception of the criteria for allocation of rewards. Strategies for influencing a given individual can then be devised in terms of the ability of the organization to offer rewards.

Work Flow. The fifth aspect of organization structure to be considered is the flow of work among positions in the organization. Figure 5–2 illustrates the nature of the work flow involved in a purchasing action, although step 2 in that illustration is the only stage involving a buying "decision" in the sense that we have been using that term. The illustration is useful, however, in suggesting the flow of paperwork, the procedures, and the people involved in the organizational buying process.

There are important interdependencies between the flow of work and the interaction of people in the organization. To the extent that the work flow is specified by the formal organization structure, it can be thought of as a major determinant of the nature of interpersonal interaction. Conversely, to the extent that people exercise their own volition in determining the nature of their interpersonal interaction, the flow of work is likely to be modified in a manner reflecting these interactions. Studies have found that work flow influences the attitudes of organizational actors toward one another; to the extent that the flow of work brings people into contact with each other, they are likely to develop feelings of affection toward each other.

To summarize quickly, five aspects of organization structure have been examined as they influence the organizational buying process: communication, authority, status, rewards, and work flow. Having considered the influence of the buying task and of the organization structure, we next consider the influence of technology on the functioning of the buying organization.

BUYING TECHNOLOGY

We saw in Chapter 4 that technology has its impact both on what is bought and on the nature of the buying process itself. Technology includes the physical plant and equipment owned and used by the organization; it also includes the programs and procedures used to manage the enterprise, and the various systems that are put in place to facilitate the functioning of the organization.

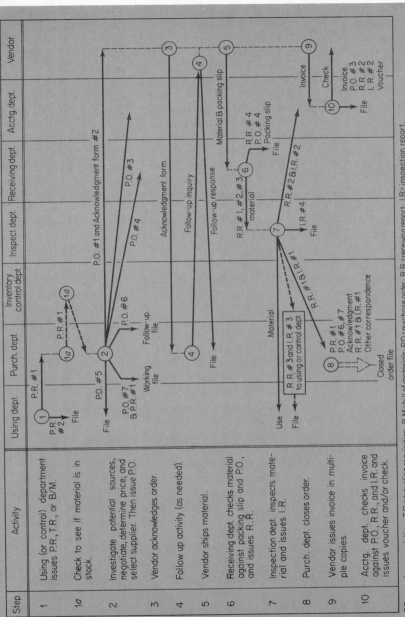

FIGURE 5-2. An Illustration of Work Flow in Buying Organizations

Reproduced, with permission, from Lamar Lee, Jr., and Donald W. Dobler, Purchasing and Materials Management (New York: McGraw-Hill Book Company, Inc., 1965), p. 419.

Some organizations are much more advanced than others in the application of management science techniques to the buying process. These techniques include inventory control models, computer programs for determining optimum order quantities, value analysis methods, PERT (Program Evaluation and Review Technique) charts for scheduling major purchases, the development of forecasting models for predicting important price changes, and computer routines for comparing buying alternatives. Computers have found their way into the buying process not only as the handmaidens of management science but also as devices for routinizing much organizational buying and even, with appropriate communication devices, for connecting organizations directly with their suppliers and making order decisions and handling subsequent invoicing and other activities, especially for staple items that can be replenished routinely. Typically the computer and management science (or operations research) go hand-in-hand.

Despite the potential value of these and other applications of operations research to organizational purchasing, most organizations do not utilize these techniques, limiting their "scientific" work to inventory control models and value analysis.

There is no longer any doubt that management science and the computer will find increasing usage in all organizational decision making. The major barriers at this time seem to be in communication; the decision-makers and the management scientists seldom speak the same language or think about problems in the same way. This situation will change as young men and women trained in professional schools of management find their way into organizations. In the meantime, most buying organizations will continue to rely upon simple systems for directing and controlling the buying process. Manually maintained inventory records, manually written purchase orders, and laborious calculations to compare alternative bids are all part of the typical buying operation at the moment.

On the positive side, however, organization technology influences the buying decision by defining the technological constraints within which current decisions must be made. Current plant and equipment place a significant boundary around the set of alternative buying actions that can be considered at any moment. The equipment in a factory will determine the kind of raw materials that can be used in the manufacturing process; the physical construction of a laboratory will be a major determinant of the kind of equipment that can be purchased; the wiring in an educational building may be an important consideration in the purchase of audio-visual aids, and so on. Furthermore, certain purchasing actions may be avoided either because they will make existing plant and equipment obsolete or because they will require significant new investment in other equipment or in modifications of the physical plant. This fact often has been overlooked by marketing managers with new products to sell to organizations. Any new product or service must fit into a system of technology that the buying organization already has in use. To charge ahead with a selling effort without an adequate understanding of the organizational technology in potential customer organizations is to invite costly failure and inefficient marketing strategies.

BUYING CENTER

We have earlier defined the people of the organization who are involved in the buying process as the buying center. The individual actors involved in the buying process are certainly a major determinant in the organizational buying process, both as individuals and as a social group whose members interact with one another and who develop norms, sanctions, and other devices for influencing members' behavior. Although Chapters 6 and 7 are devoted exclusively to the "people" dimension of organizational buying behavior, the interactive and interdependent nature of the total organization nevertheless should be stressed here. People do not operate only as individuals or even only as members of the social group of other organizational members. Their behavior and the results of their behavior are heavily influenced by the other organizational systems of technology, structure, and communication.

This "systems" aspect of organizational behavior (i.e., the interdependent nature of each of the organization's components) has tremendous implications for any attempts to change the behavior of people within an organization. Two broad classes of strategies are available to an agent attempting to bring about change. He may try to influence the behavior of the people directly through communication—information, commands, instructions, persuasion, and so on; or he may attempt to manipulate other organizational variables—technology, structure (authority, status, rewards, and work flows) or tasks—in order to influence the behavior of individuals indirectly.

Similar choices are, theoretically at least, available to the marketer who wishes to influence organizational buying behavior. He can try to deal directly with the individual members of the buying center and attempt to persuade them to purchase his offering, or he can attempt to alter the organization in some indirect manner in such a way as to enhance his chances of making a sale.

We have seen, then, that the organization is defined by four subsystems —tasks, structure, technology, and people. Structure includes not only the hierarchical structure of statuses that is characteristic of all formal organizations but also the communication, authority, rewards, and work flow systems that provide important substance to the organization. This review of the nature and scope of organizational variables has defined many classes of variables, examined their interactions, and suggested their importance as determinants of organizational buying behavior. The marketing strategist who hopes to persuade organizations to buy has the responsibility for defining and understanding the nature of these variables in the context of the specific organization he is trying to influence. Here we can only build the skeleton of an analytical structure. The strategist must measure each of these factors and assess its implications for his specific situation.

Locus of Buying Responsibility

The organization itself is too big a target for marketing effort except at the very early stages of contact. The marketer must identify those individuals within the organization who have either formal or informal responsibility and authority for buying decisions and who must be persuaded as part of the selling task. The problem is to define the locus of buying responsibility within the customer organization, to define the membership of the buying center, and to understand the structure of roles and authority within the buying center.

EFFECTS OF CENTRALIZATION AND DECENTRALIZATION

There is almost always some one individual within the formal organization who has ultimate responsibility and authority for the purchasing function, although this may only involve one or a few stages of the total buying process—typically the selection of suppliers to meet predetermined specifications. The specific nature of the centralized responsibility will reflect the reasons for centralization and the nature of the organization's operations. Centralization is typically motivated by a combination of factors, which is most likely to include the desire to achieve economies through purchasing larger quantities, the desire for some degree of consistency and control within disparate purchasing operations, and the desire to direct specialized management expertise to this class of problems.

When the organization consists of separate autonomous units, however, as in the case of a multi-plant manufacturing operation, some degree of decentralization is highly likely. Decentralization may be necessary because of differences in local market conditions, the need for quick reaction to changes in market situations, or the need to buy from nearby sources to minimize transportation costs. Decentralization also may be required by the basic organizational philosophy of the company. In a truly autonomous unit where the local manager has profit responsibility for the performance of his unit, he must have control over those factors which influence profitability, including the purchase of materials from outside suppliers. On the other hand, he may be able to realize cost savings and greater profits by pooling his purchasing with that of other units in order to obtain the lower prices associated with larger quantities and other bargaining advantages. In addition, decentralization may reflect the disparate nature of different operations within the total organization, as when two divisions of the same company make different products and buy entirely different raw materials.

A common situation is to have an arrangement combining decentralization with some degree of centralization. In this situation a staff manager for purchasing reports to the chief executive and is available at the request of operating divisions to help them with their problems. The "national" or "corporate" purchasing manager may negotiate contracts with suppliers for products that are common to many divisions and may advise division purchasing officials concerning the organization and operation of their departments. He may help them develop policies and procedures, for example, or assist in the development of a computer-based purchasing system. Centralized purchasing can also perform an important information function for subsidiaries, informing them of new products and vendors, alternative sources of supply, expected changes in prices and market conditions for key raw materials, and so on. Furthermore, they can assist in orderly vendor relations by developing common, equitable policies for all divisions in such matters as acceptable credit and delivery terms, negotiation of major contracts, assistance in vendor's market research activities, and so on.

One of the authors developed and tested a conceptual framework within which to examine the effects of centralization versus decentralization on the behavior of buyers who have formal buying responsibility in the purchasing department. Centralization influences five elements of the buyer's job:

1. the geographical location of the buyer;
2. the authority relationships between buyers and users (including allocation, criteria, sampling, evaluation, and authority reversal rights, as defined earlier in this chapter);
3. The authority relationships between the buyer and the top purchasing executive (including all rights mentioned in item 2 above except authority reversal rights);
4. informal relationships between buyers and users;
5. the formal nature of communication between buyers and users.

It was hypothesized that the formal position of the buyer within the organization on the centralized-decentralized continuum would be reflected primarily in the buyer's "loyalty domain," defined as his sentiments and loyalties toward various organizational members. In other words, the organization structure influences the behavior of the buyer primarily through determining his "loyalty domain" and the distribution of social and organizational rewards to him; buyers would be expected to have more favorable attitudes toward those who were in their loyalty domain. For example, it was hypothesized that in a centralized purchasing operation the buyer's loyalty domain would be primarily in the purchasing group, where formal rewards were given by the purchasing manager and social rewards by other buyers. In a decentralized operation, on the other hand, the buyer would feel more loyal to users than to the purchasing department because of his closer proximity to users and his more frequent contact with them, both formally and informally, as well as because the users were in a better position to offer him important social rewards and to formally evaluate and reward his performance. Obviously, it follows that decentralized purchasing responsibility is more likely to be responsive to users' needs. Underlying this view of the effects of decentralization on buyer behavior was a "reward-balance" model, which asserted that a buyer's behavior is directed toward satisfying the objectives that he perceives as being the critical ones in the evaluation of his performance by his superior and hence in the rewards he receives. This model relates the organization structural systems of status, authority, reward, and communication in an explanation of the influence of structure on buyer behavior. Results of field studies supported these hypotheses and the model seems to be consistent with actual practice.[8]

The marketer would do well to consider both how the degree of centralization in the customer organization is likely to influence the buyer's loyalty domain and the effects of various criteria in determining his buying behavior. If the purchasing manager is a primary influence in the buyer's loyalty domain, for example, the buyer is likely to seek cost savings in his buying and a minimum possibility of negative feedback from users. If design or development engineers are in the loyalty domain, the buyer is likely to seek high product quality and rapid delivery in his purchasing. When manufacturing engineers are in the loyalty domain, the buyer is likely to be motivated by his perception that reliable, but not necessarily fast, delivery and cost savings are most important to them.[9] A first step in approaching the organizational customer is to understand the nature of centralization in the purchasing department and to investigate the influence of centralization on the distribution of rewards to those charged with formal responsibility for buying.

COMPOSITION OF THE BUYING CENTER

In addition to understanding the nature of centralization of purchasing responsibility within the organization, the marketer must identify those other organizational actors who comprise the buying center along with members of the purchasing department.

The composition of the buying center will vary according to the buying situation and will be determined primarily by the nature of the buying task and by the interaction of the communication and authority systems of the organizational structure. The one common element is likely to be representation of the purchasing department in the buying center; other roles will be determined by what is being purchased. The larger the amount of expenditure involved and the more critical the buying decision to the total operation of the organization, the more likely that top management personnel will be involved in the buying center. Most organizations make

[8] Yoram Wind, "Industrial Buying Behavior: Source Loyalty in the Purchase of Industrial Components," unpublished Ph.D. dissertation, Graduate School of Business, Stanford University, 1966.

[9] Yoram Wind, "A Reward-Balance Model of Buying Behavior in Organizations," in George Fisk, ed., *New Essays in Marketing Theory* (Boston: Allyn & Bacon, Inc., 1971).

provision for including top management in all decisions involving expenditures of more than a specified dollar amount, at least to the extent of requiring executive authorization of the expenditure.

Common sense can help in predicting the identity of members of the buying center. If the offered product is likely to influence the marketability of the customer's products, then the sales and marketing people of the customer organization are likely to be involved. If capital expenditures will be involved, then financial executives will have an influence. If the purchased materials are used in the production process, then design engineering and manufacturing personnel will be included as influencers and deciders in the buying center.

It is often possible for the marketer to influence the composition of the buying center, and it may be to his advantage to do so. For example, the true benefits of a product may be discernible only to those who actually use a product. An automatic typewriter may offer benefits that only a secretary can truly understand although the buyer might be frightened by the high cost involved and unable to understand the value offered by the product in use. The seller is always well advised to make sure via his promotional strategy that those who stand to benefit most from using the product are actively involved in the buying center. This is especially the case where the product or service being offered has a higher price than its substitutes; value must be created through careful explanation of product benefits to those who can appreciate them and who will derive personal benefit from them.

Another problem for the marketer is to determine the relative power of members of the buying center and, specifically, who has ultimate buying responsibility—that is, who are the deciders. Having identified deciders, it is also necessary to identify those influencers who are most likely to have an effect on the deciders. It is often the case that ultimate decision responsibility is left with a manager at a high level in the organization, but his actual involvement may be minimal. He will rely upon the advice of those organizational members who seem to him best qualified to make the necessary judgments about what is needed and the ability of alternative vendors to meet those criteria. These people may in turn be influenced by the judgments of members of their staffs. The result is that key influencers, those who will be the best targets for marketing effort and product information, are likely to be quite low in the organizational hierarchy. Seldom are these relationships obvious at first glance. Rather, the marketer must specifically attempt to get information to identify the composition as it influences the functioning of the buying center.

The Behavioral Theory of the Firm

To this point we have concerned ourselves exclusively with the formal structure of the organization. Recognizing that the interpersonal and individual behavior of organizational members is a key determinant of organizational performance, we have repeatedly postponed discussion of these obviously important factors for later chapters. The purpose of this final section is to build a conceptual bridge between the formal organization and the individuals who act within it.

The organization, as we have seen, exerts a powerful influence on the actions of individuals who operate within it, but this should not obscure the fact that the individuals also exert a powerful influence on the organization. An organization without people is a hollow structure, completely incapable of action.

The so-called "behavioral theory of the firm" has made a major contribution to our understanding of organizational behavior by specifically recognizing how the sociopsychological mechanisms of individual behavior determine organizational functioning. This conceptual approach was developed by members of the faculty of the Graduate School of Industrial Administration at the Carnegie Institute of Technology (now Carnegie-Mellon University) in the late 1950s and early 1960s. Its principal architects have been Professors Herbert Simon, Richard Cyert, James March, and William Dill, along with many of their doctoral students.[10] The distinctive contribution of this theory has been its replacement of traditional concepts of how organizations are supposed to operate (principally the classical economic theory of the firm with its rationality and profit maximization assumptions) by explanations of how organizations actually do operate, based on empirical studies of decision making within the organization. It is our judgment that the behavioral theory of the firm offers one of the richest and most realistic frameworks for understanding the nature of organizational buying behavior.

The behavioral theory of the firm consists of three subtheories: (1) a theory of organizational goal-setting; (2) a theory of organizational expectations including a theory of search); and (3) a theory of organizational choice. The building blocks of these three theories are four relational concepts, briefly described as follows:

> 1. *Quasi resolution of conflict*—there is latent conflict among goals in most organizations.[11] This conflict must be resolved by finding some kind of consensus among organizational members. Goals are seen as a series of independent aspiration-level constraints imposed on the organization by members of the organization, who are regarded as a coalition motivated by common purposes that are more likely to be realized by cooperative action. Three mechanisms are used to reduce goal conflict:
>   a. *local rationality*—problems are broken into subproblems and dealt with by subunits of the organization,

[10] For the most comprehensive statement of this theory, see Richard M. Cyert and James G. March, *A Behavioral Theory of the Firm* (Englewood Cliffs, N.J.: Prentice-Hall, Inc., 1963).

[11] Goals are affected by two sets of variables in the behavioral theory of the firm: the first set of variables influences the *dimensions* of the goals, the things which are regarded as important by the organization; the second set of variables influences the *aspiration level* of any goal dimension. Aspiration level is believed to be determined by three variables: the organization's past goal, its past performance, and the past performance of other comparable or competing organizations.

which are in turn concerned with only a subset of organizational goals. Delegation and specialization are thus used to make simple problems out of complex problems.

b. *acceptable level decision rules*—organizational actors do not look for the best decision but for one which is merely acceptable within the constraints of organizational goals and subgoals. Given local rationality, it is likely that the resulting decisions will be suboptimal for the total organization. The resulting sets of decisions will tend to "underexploit" the environment and will leave opportunities for improvement as well as some excess organizational resources to absorb the potential inconsistencies in local decisions.

c. *sequential attention to goals*—problems tend to be approached one at a time. For example, a business firm is likely to fluctuate between the goal of reducing costs by smoothing production, reducing inventories, eliminating marginal accounts etc. and the goal of creating satisfied customers through providing better (and more expensive) service. The result of sequential attention to goals is to put a buffer between conflicting goals.

2. *Uncertainty avoidance*—organizational actors are motivated by a desire to reduce uncertainty. This contributes to a tendency to devote attention to short-term problems permitting faster feedback of results and to avoid long-range problem solving and planning. The desire to reduce uncertainty also produces a "negotiated environment," a set of relationships with the environment worked out through planning, procedures, contractual relationships with suppliers, and following traditional practices. Standard operating procedure, traditional industry practice (as regards price setting, for example), and contracts with suppliers and customers are all parts of the negotiated environment. Rather than predict the environment, the attempt is to control it.

3. *Problemistic search*—the search for information is caused by definition of a problem and is directed at solving that problem. (It is neither random curiosity nor search for understanding.) The rate of search activity is increased by problem definition and reduced by problem solution. Search is said to be "simple-minded" in that it is usually based on very simple models of the causal relationships involved in the definition of the problem. Search tends to be located in the neighborhood of the symptoms of the problem and in the neighborhood of currently known solutions to similar problems. The direction of search, then, is from the familiar to the less familiar until an acceptable course of action is found. This tendency inhibits innovation in the organization. When search using simple rules is not

successful, it is extended to unfamiliar areas, to the consideration of new alternatives, and to parts of the organization that are "vulnerable" and where organizational "slack" is likely to exist. Organizational areas where the connection to major goals is less direct (such as "research") are likely to be most vulnerable. Finally, search is also said to be "biased" in that the direction of search is likely to reflect specialization and past experience, the hopes and expectations of the searchers, and the unresolved conflicts within the organization.

4. *Organizational learning*—like individuals, organizations exhibit adaptive behavior over time. Three kinds of adaptive behavior are significant:

   a. *adaptation of goals*—goals are adjusted upward or downward to reflect success or failure in achieving the previous period's goals and the performance of comparable organizations. Some organizations are more sensitive to the performance of comparable organizations than others.

   b. *adaptation in attention rules*—organizations learn which parts of the environment to pay attention to. In evaluation, organizations learn to pay attention to some criteria and to ignore others. They also learn to pay attention to some comparable organizations and to ignore others, and to pay attention to only some components of performance within comparable organizations.

   c. *adaptation in search rules*—search rules change to reflect success and failure. When a solution is found in one area, search will likely come back to that area in the future.

In terms of its decision-making implications, the behavioral theory of the firm sees organizations as coalitions whose members tend to simplify problems by subdividing them, to look for solutions that are acceptable but not necessarily optimal, to deal with problems on a one-at-a-time basis, to avoid uncertainty by establishing reliable relationships, to look for familiar solutions to problems, to look for solutions consistent with previous experience and expectations, and to change behavior to reflect success and failure in accomplishing previous goals and solving previous problems. The organizational decision process is continuous in that it is "started" by feedback on the results of previous decisions.[12] A flow chart of the organizational decision process summarizing these basic features of the behavioral theory of the firm is presented in Figure 5–3.

EMPIRICAL FINDINGS

Both of the present authors have conducted studies that support the notion that the behavioral theory of the firm can be of real value in understand-

[12] Cyert and March, *op. cit.*, 114–27.

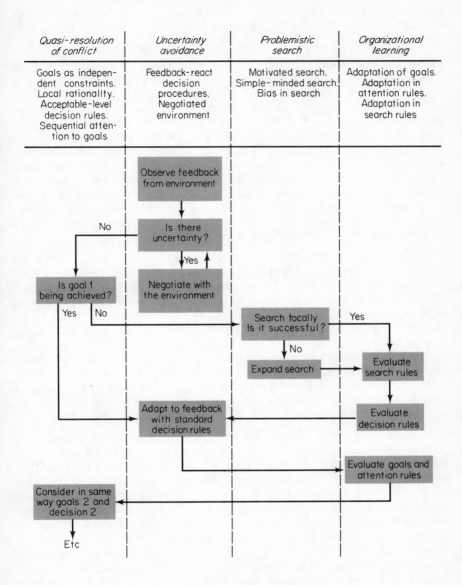

FIGURE 5–3.   A Summary of the Behavioral Theory of the Firm

Reproduced, with permission, from Richard M. Cyert and James G. March, A Behavioral Theory of the Firm (Englewood Cliffs, N.J.: Prentice-Hall Inc., 1963), p. 126.

ing the organizational buying decision process.[13] Some of the more important findings about organizational buying behavior in terms of the concepts
of the behavioral theory of the firm are presented in the following pages.

Quasi-Resolution of Conflict. Examples of latent conflict of goals can
be found among the members of every buying center, reflecting their
specialized interests and responsibilities within the organization, as well as
their personal needs and wishes. To a large extent, the nature of the individual's goals will reflect, and can be predicted from, his position within
the organization. Thus, the decision criteria used by members of the buying center can be intelligently guessed on the basis of whether they are
members of the purchasing department, engineers, production people,
financial control personnel, and so on. Procedures for obtaining local
rationality are reflected in the organizational assignment of authority and
responsibility for the stages of the buying decision process. Also, the
buyer may try to resolve conflict by favoring some organizational members
in one instance and others in other instances, as suggested by the concept
of sequential attention to goals.

Uncertainty Avoidance. The organizational buying process is by its
very nature an example of an attempt to avoid uncertainty through creating
a negotiated environment. Buyers exhibit a definite tendency to favor
known suppliers and to do business with reliable suppliers. The risks of
innovation are avoided and the willingness of an organizational buyer to
innovate, or his ability to tolerate risk in his decision making, reflects
among other things his recent experience and whether his goal levels are
increasing, static, or decreasing. Another strategy used by organizational
buyers to reduce risk is to split orders between two or more vendors,
although single sourcing (especially from well-known suppliers) was
found to be a more common practice in the specific case of industrial
electronic components.

Problemistic Search. Buyers avoid consideration of new alternatives as
long as things are going well. New alternatives are considered only where
problems are created, as when goal attainment falls below acceptable
levels either because goals significantly change or because vendor performance falls. Buyers are busy and allocate their scarce time resources to those
problems that seem most urgent or most easily solved. There often is no
attempt to identify all possible alternative courses of action and to choose
the best one. Rather, the search is for an acceptable alternative. Having
found a workable solution to his problem, the busy buyer is likely to go on
to another problem instead of searching for a better solution to this problem. Also, buyers definitely consider familiar alternatives first. The need
for something new usually stimulates a search with other organizational
members (users or buyers), with present suppliers, or for suppliers in the

[13] Frederick E. Webster, Jr., "Modeling the Industrial Buying Process,"
Journal of Marketing Research, II (November 1965), 370–76; Yoram Wind, "Applying the Behavioral Theory of the Firm to Industrial Buying Decisions," *The Economic and Business Bulletin,* XX (Spring 1968), 22–28.

local area. Only when this fails will new alternative suppliers be considered, and these are usually identified by seeking the assistance of buyers in organizations that are geographically nearby.[14]

Organizational Learning. All three aspects of organizational learning have been observed in our studies of organizational buying. Goals will be modified upward or downward to reflect success or failure in previous periods and to reflect success or failure in search. If no acceptable alternatives are identified in search, the buyer may either change the goals, making one or more of the previously defined alternatives now acceptable, or he may modify his search rules hoping to identify new alternatives that will be acceptable to present goal aspirations. Furthermore, as indicated above, the buyer is busy and allocates his time according to the notions of adaptation in attention rules. He pays attention to those problems that require attention most urgently. As noted in our discussion of the reward-balance model, the buyer's selectivity in his attention to evaluation criteria depends upon his previous experience with rewards. Buying behavior that is successful in terms of solving problems and earning rewards tends to be repeated. Satisfactory product performance results in repeat orders, and a vendor who can supply one needed product is very likely to be subsequently called upon for other products as well.

The behavioral theory of the firm thus provides a dynamic model of organizational behavior that is relevant for the study of organizational buying and produces some insights into the specific ways in which individuals influence organizational performance. Within the framework of the formal organization, individual members of the buying center influence organizational functioning through a set of mechanisms for reducing goal conflict, avoiding uncertainty, searching for solutions to problems in the easiest fashion, and adjusting their behavior to reflect their experience. It is the "quasi-rational" buyer, looking for satisfactory solutions to those subproblems for which he is responsible, who makes the organization work.

Summary

Our approach to a consideration of the impact of organizational factors on the buying process has consisted of three parts. First, we examined the formal organization, identifying four interacting systems of organizational variables—tasks, structure, technology, and people. Organizational structure was in turn broken into five sets of factors: communication, authority, status, reward, and work-flow systems. Each of these sets of variables was considered in terms of its influence on the buying decision and it was stressed that all of these systems interact in complex ways to determine final buying action.

The question of the locus of buying responsibility within the organization was next approached by considering the specific question of degree of centralization of the purchasing function. The concept of the buyer's

---

[14] Frederick E. Webster, Jr., "Informal Communication in Industrial Markets," *Journal of Marketing Research*, VII (May 1970), 186–89.

loyalty domain was introduced as a way of thinking about the influence of various degrees of centralization and, consistent with a reward-balance model, it was seen that buyer's behavior is influenced by the way in which the various organizational systems interact to determine the formal and social rewards available to the buyer. We also considered the question of the composition of the buying center and the relative influence of various members on the buying decision process.

Finally, we have considered the behavioral theory of the firm with its assertions about four mechanisms of decision making which seem to lend particular insight into the way in which people influence organizational functioning. Because the behavioral theory of the firm is dynamic and is based upon actual observation of decision making in formal organizations, it has direct relevance for our understanding of the influence of organizational factors on the organizational buying process.

INTERPERSONAL INFLUENCES IN ORGANIZATIONAL BUYING

The people involved in organizational buying decisions *interact* with one another, sharing knowledge and attempting to influence the outcome of the process to their advantage. The nature of these interpersonal interactions is the subject of this chapter.

Although it is hard in actual buying situations to separate the influence of other persons within the buying organization from the influence of the organization itself, such a distinction can be made for purposes of analysis. It must be borne in mind, however, that individual, interpersonal, organizational, and environmental influences interact and simultaneously shape organizational buying behavior.

Interpersonal influence is defined simply as the influence of one person on another. When several individuals interact simultaneously and are guided by a shared set of objectives, norms, expectations, and so on, interpersonal influences become "group" influences. The term "interpersonal" is used in this chapter because it includes both dyadic interaction (between two people) and the broader category of group influence.

Given the broad scope of interpersonal relations and the rich behavioral science literature on small groups and interpersonal behavior, the purpose of this chapter is to suggest some of the key interpersonal influences on organizational buying decisions. Starting with a brief review of the nature and scope of interpersonal relations, the focus of the chapter will be on the two major forms of interpersonal influences on buying decisions—the relations among members of the buying center and the performance of buying committees.

The Nature and Scope of Interpersonal Relations

Both the sociological and social psychological literature are characterized by a variety of small group and interpersonal behavior models and hypotheses. Quasi-mechanical, organismic, structural-functional, and cybernetic-growth models are only a few of the models which have been developed to explain small group and interpersonal behavior.[1] At a finer level of analysis, the driving forces of the communicative interaction among members of any group have been hypothesized in terms of bargaining and the exchange of rewarding things and events (exchange theory [2]); normative cooperation or compliance with stabilized expectations (consensus theory [3]); maintenance of congruency of relations under changing conditions (homeostasis model [4]); communication of information, instruction, or motivation in a meeting of purposive minds (behavioral theory of communication [5]); and maximizing of payoffs or playing strategies (game theory [6]). All of these models [7] deal with "a system of interlinked components that can only be defined in terms of the interrelations of each of them in an on-going developmental process that generates emergent phenomena." [8]

Whereas the component units of these various theories can be seen as individuals who participate in, rather than belong to, any given group, a more common approach is to view the system as made up of roles. According to this approach, groups can be seen as role systems which include role expectations (prescriptions and prohibitions associated with the given role), role behavior (the actual behavior of a given person in a given role), and role relationships (the multiple and reciprocal relationship of the members of the group). The pattern of role relationships then can be referred to as the group structure.[9] Yet this structure of role relationships is only one of numerous variables affecting the outcome of interpersonal behavior. A more comprehensive model of interpersonal behavior is presented in Figure 6–1. The model, although necessarily an oversimplification, emphasizes a number of key factors: (1) the multiplicity of and interdependency among the factors affecting group processes and outcomes; (2) the fact that the essence of a group process can be described as the mutual relationships among activities, interactions, and senti-

[1] For a discussion of these and other models, see Theodore M. Mills, *The Sociology of Small Groups* (Englewood Cliffs, N.J.: Prentice-Hall, Inc., 1967).

[2] George C. Homans, *Social Behavior: Its Elementary Forms* (New York: Harcourt Brace Jovanovich, Inc., 1961).

[3] Talcott Parsons, *The Social System* (New York: The Free Press, 1951).

[4] Theodore M. Newcomb, "An Approach to the Study of Communicative Acts," *Psychological Review*, LX (1953), 393–404.

[5] Russell L. Ackoff, "Towards a Behavioral Theory of Communication," *Management Science* (April 1958), 218–34.

[6] Anatol Rapoport, "Game Theory and Human Conflict," in E. B. McNeil, ed., *The Nature of Human Conflict* (Englewood Cliffs, N.J.: Prentice-Hall, Inc., 1965).

[7] For a critical review of these models see Walter Buckley, *Sociology and Modern Systems Theory* (Englewood Cliffs, N.J.: Prentice-Hall, Inc., 1967).

[8] *Ibid.*, 125.

[9] Joseph E. McGrath, *Social Psychology: A Brief Introduction* (New York: Holt, Rinehart & Winston, Inc., 1964).

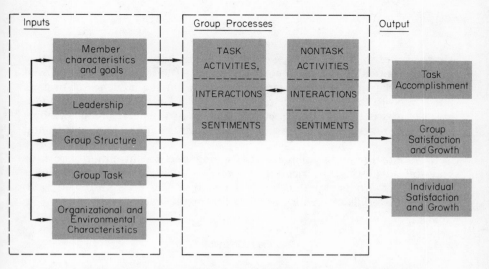

FIGURE 6–1.   A Model of Interpersonal Determinates of Buying Behavior

ments; [10] (3) the relevance of both task and nontask activities, interactions, and sentiments; and (4) the nature of the output (consequences) of the group process, which includes not only the accomplishment of the task but also the satisfaction and growth of both the group and the individual.

The Buying Center

Members of the organization who interact during the buying decision process can be defined as the buying center. There are several distinct roles in the buying center: users, influencers, buyers, deciders, and gatekeepers. Understanding these roles will help one understand the nature of interpersonal influence in the buying decision process. It is quite likely that several individuals will occupy the same role within the buying center (e.g., there may be several users) and that one individual may occupy two or more roles (e.g., buyer and gatekeeper). All members of the buying center can be seen as influencers, but not all influencers occupy other roles.

[10] For a detailed analysis of these basic small group concepts, see Anthony G. Athos and Robert E. Coffey, *Behavior in Organizations: A Multidimensional View* (Englewood Cliffs, N.J.: Prentice-Hall, Inc., 1968).

USERS

Users may exert their influence either individually or collectively. In many cases the potential users are those who initiate the buying process or even formulate the specific purchase requirements, but the influence of users is not limited to these particular roles. The performance of purchased goods and services is often the subject for labor grievances and union members may band together to influence specifications for purchased goods and services.

Users can therefore influence the buying decision in either a positive way—by suggesting the need for purchased materials and by defining standards of product quality—or in a negative way—by refusing to work with the materials of certain suppliers for any of several reasons.

INFLUENCERS

Influencers are organizational members who directly or indirectly influence buying or usage decisions. Typically, they exert their influence either by defining criteria which constrain the choices that can be considered in the purchase decision or by providing information with which to evaluate alternative buying actions.

In manufacturing organizations, technical personnel are known to be significant influencers of the purchasing decision, especially in situations involving the development of new products to be manufactured by the buying organization and in the purchase of equipment to be used in the production process, especially where new technologies are involved. Likewise, production scheduling may become an important influence at the purchase scheduling stage. Research and development personnel, design engineering, production engineering, and manufacturing management may all exert significant influence and may emphasize different factors to be considered in the buying decision. Their principal influence may be to define what is to be purchased and the technical (and perhaps economic) criteria that must be met by purchased parts.

BUYERS

Buyers are those organizational members with formal authority for selecting the supplier and arranging the terms of the purchase. Depending upon the nature of the formal organization and its size, buyers may have such titles as Purchasing Manager, Purchasing Agent, or Buyer, or this responsibility and authority may reside with people other than those designated specifically as buyers, a vice president-manufacturing, an office manager, or some other official, for example.

Although the buyer may have formal authority for negotiating with suppliers and for committing the organization to supply contracts, the choices available to him may be significantly limited by the formal and informal influence of others. For example, technical personnel may have authority for establishing specifications and may do so in a manner which forces the buyer to deal with a particular supplier.

The influence of the buyer comes at various stages of the buying decision process but is especially apparent in determining the set of feasible suppliers and in selecting the suppliers. The buyer's influence depends, of course, on the nature of the buying task. It can be a relatively routine decision process of applying previously established criteria to a limited range of acceptable alternatives, a function that is essentially clerical in nature; or it may be somewhat more complex if there is the need to negotiate prices and other conditions of sale as part of the process of arranging the purchase contract. It is most complex when it involves simultaneously defining specifications and evaluating available alternatives to determine the most economical way of solving the buying problem.

DECIDERS

Deciders are those members of the organization who have either formal or informal power to determine the final selection of suppliers. The buyer may be the decider, but it is also possible that the buying decision actually will be made by somebody else and left to the buyer for implementation.

In actual practice it is not always easy to determine when the decision is actually made and who actually makes it. A *de facto* buying decision may be made by the development engineer who, knowing or unknowingly, develops a specification that can be met by only one supplier. Thus, although the purchasing agent may be the only person with formal authority to sign a buying contract, he may not be the true decider.

Many purchasing agents' job descriptions actually place an upper limit on the financial commitments that they can make, reserving larger decisions for other members of the organization such as a vice president or the president or even the board of directors.

GATEKEEPERS

Gatekeepers are group members who control the flow of information into the group. Perhaps the best example of a gatekeeper in a formal organization is the purchasing agent or buyer who has formal responsibility and authority for managing the relationships of the firm with vendors and potential vendors. In such a situation the buyer may have formal authority for allowing salesmen to call upon the engineering department or may be responsible for maintaining a library of catalogues.

Purchasing agents are not the only gatekeepers in the organization, however. Salesmen employed by the buying organization can be a significant source of information about the availability of products and services in the market. General management also may be exposed to important sources of information, and technical personnel especially are likely to be exposed to information about new products and new technology of interest to the firm.

Gatekeepers exert their influence primarily at the stage of identifying buying alternatives. Because they actively influence the definition of the feasible set of buying alternatives, they significantly determine the outcome of the purchase decision. Table 6–1 defines the most likely influences of

TABLE 6–1. Decision Stages and Roles in the Buying Center

	User	Influencer	Buyer	Decider	Gate-keeper
Identification of Need	X	X			
Establishing Specifications and Scheduling the Purchase	X	X	X	X	
Identifying Buying Alternatives	X	X	X		X
Evaluating Alternative Buying Actions	X	X	X		
Selecting the Suppliers	X	X	X	X	

members of the buying center at each of the five stages of the buying decision process.

Relationships in the Buying Center

Relationships among members of the buying center reflect a complex interaction of personal and organizational goals that direct the performance of organizational members. In Chapter 7 the nature of the relationship between personal and organizational goals will be explored more fully as these determine the way each organizational member plays his role and the expectations that he has for other members of the organization; here we will note only that individual and organizational goals combine in unique ways to determine a "frame of reference" or "point of view" that guides each individual and determines his interpretation of the behavior of other members of the buying center. The individual's frame of reference determines the criteria he will use in evaluating alternative buying actions (products and suppliers), his attitudes toward other members of the buying center, his expectations for salesmen, as well as his exposure to other sources of buying information.

The focus of the following remarks is the buyer—the person in the organization with formal authority for the selection of sources of supply. Although this authority may be constrained in many important ways, it is in many cases the key *terminal* position of organizational responsibility for the buying decision. In other words, the buyer (or purchasing agent) is the final decision-maker, so that when other members of the buying center attempt to exert influence, their efforts are directed toward him with the intention of constraining or otherwise influencing the choices available to him.

BUYERS' FUNCTIONS

In his formal buying responsibilities, the purchasing agent is typically responsible for six organizational functions. First, he is responsible for negotiating prices and other terms of sale with vendors. Second, he is responsible for generating alternative solutions to the buying problem and keeping organization members informed of market conditions. Third, he is responsible for protecting the organization's cost structure, especially as it is influenced by the prices paid for purchased goods and services and more generally as it is influenced by the effect of purchased goods and services on the costs of performing the work of the organization. Fourth, he is responsible for assuring long-term sources of supply for those goods and services necessary for organization functioning. Fifth, he has responsibility for the general maintenance of good relationships with suppliers. Sixth, he must manage the mechanics of the procurement process, including establishing reorder points on routinely purchased items, placing orders with suppliers, expediting orders, checking orders when received, maintaining records of transactions with suppliers, and so forth.[11]

Other members of the organization have different functions, different objectives, and different criteria for evaluating alternative buying actions. The objectives and criteria used by an organization member will reflect many factors, including the personality characteristics of the individual, his involvement in previous buying decisions, and (some would say, most significantly) the criteria that are used to judge that individual's performance in the organization.

Each member of the organization will evaluate alternative buying actions according to the extent to which they will contribute to his performance in the organization and enhance it in some way, such as by making it more effective or easier.

In order to perform his functions most effectively, the purchasing agent typically feels that he must be involved in the decision process at the earliest stages—that is, at the stage of defining the need for purchased

[11] Patrick J. Robinson, Charles W. Faris, and Yoram Wind, *Industrial Buying and Creative Marketing* (Boston: Allyn & Bacon, Inc., 1967), 135–37.

products or services. He wants to participate actively in the determination of specifications and in the identification of alternative buying actions. He wants to avoid specifications or delivery requirements that unduly limit the number of alternatives that can be considered, in order to assure that the best value is received from available alternatives in the marketplace.

Especially if the buyer is ambitious, he will want to achieve management recognition and enhanced status within the organization and, identifying with the profession of purchasing, he will actively seek to enlarge the scope of his authority and responsibility. He will actively fight any tendency to keep the purchasing function from being involved before the final stages of placing orders and he will resist specifications that limit the alternatives that he can consider. The purchasing agent's ambitions and desires for increased status cause disequilibrium and upset the stability of his relationships with other members of the buying center. Instead of being on the "receiving" end of the purchasing decision process, where requisitions are given to him for routine clerical attention, he tries to make the interactions flow both ways by encouraging people to accept his advice, information, and guidance as they define specifications, set schedules, evaluate vendors, and so on.[12] He wants involvement at all stages of the buying decision.

TACTICS OF LATERAL RELATIONSHIP

The lateral relationships model was considered briefly in Chapter 2. George Strauss has studied the tactics used by purchasing agents to influence their relationships with other departments as a special case of the more general phenomenon of "lateral" relationships in formal organizations—that is, relationships among members of roughly equal status in the formal organizational hierarchy.[13] His observations suggested that purchasing agents' tactics could be categorized as follows:

1. *Rule-oriented* tactics, such as appealing to the boss for the enforcement of organizational policy (a harsh step, seldom used); appealing to rules and formal statements of authority; requiring members of the buying center to accept responsibility for their actions in writing (as when an engineer specifies a brand name); and requiring using departments to accept financial charges.

2. *Rule-evading* tactics, including complying literally with requests from users that violate organizational policies, and exceeding formal authority as when a different brand is purchased than the one specified by the using department, ordering more than policies allow, and so on.

[12] George Strauss, "Tactics of Lateral Relationship," *Administrative Science Quarterly,* VII (September 1962), 161–86.

[13] *Ibid.*

3. *Personal-political* tactics, including reliance on informal relationships and friendships to get decisions made and exchanging favors with other members of the buying center, such as agreeing to buy something for an individual's personal use or giving favored treatment (e.g., in expediting orders) to those who are cooperative. Interdepartmental politics can become significant, especially when the purchasing department is trying to enlarge its influence, as when there is a battle between purchasing and manufacturing for control of inventories or when value analysis activities are perceived as encroaching on the prerogatives of the engineering department.

4. *Educational* tactics are designed to persuade other members of the organization to think in purchasing terms. The purchasing agent may rely simply upon his knowledge of products, suppliers, and other relevant facts to directly persuade others. Or he may rely upon indirect persuasive techniques such as flattery, presenting facts and letting the other person draw his own conclusions, or carefully controlling the flow of information within the organization (the gatekeeper function). The ambitious purchasing agent may be eager to help others in the organization understand the scope, importance, and potential contribution of the purchasing function.

5. *Organizational-interactional* tactics are designed to change the formal organization structure and the pattern of reporting relationships and information flows. A formal enlargement of job responsibility and authority may be required to secure involvement of the purchasing department at earlier stages of the buying decision. Similar formal steps may be required to facilitate the interaction of buyers with other members of the organization.

Strauss found that the typical purchasing agent used a variety of tactics, depending upon the specific problems that he faced and the conditions of the organization. Some agents typically sought formal grants of authority while others preferred a more indirect form of influence. Some thought in long-range terms with a strategy for achieving desired permanent changes in the conduct of the buying process while others dealt with each conflict separately. As a generalization, it was suggested that both "expansionist" agents, seeking to enlarge the scope and influence of the purchasing function, and better educated purchasing agents were more likely to rely upon informal tactics.

SOCIAL NEGOTIATIONS

Another conceptual framework for analyzing relationships within the buying center is provided by the Walton-McKerzie model of social negotiations.[14] According to this model, any form of social negotiation is composed of four systems of activities:

1. *Distributive bargaining* resolves pure conflicts of interest between two interdependent parties. The game theorist would call such situations "constant sum" games in which a fixed payoff is to be distributed between the opponents in the contest. In the buying process such a situation may be found when one party wishes to emphasize lowest cost while another wishes to obtain maximum quality, and price and quality are highly correlated.

2. *Integrative bargaining* is an attempt to find areas of mutual interest and common concern where the parties are not in pure conflict. Integrative bargaining is not possible unless the payoffs to both parties *can* be enhanced by co-operation—in other words, integrative bargaining is *not* possible in a constant sum game. A purchasing agent engages in integrative bargaining when he attempts to demonstrate to two other buying influences how their needs can be better served by a compromise, as when production scheduling is willing to take a slight delay in delivery in order to permit manufacturing to obtain a product better suited to its needs with the result that a better combination of delivery and product quality is obtained than if only delivery had been emphasized.

3. *Attitudinal structuring* is concerned with developing the most productive social relationships among members of the social system. When the purchasing agent attempts to build a spirit of cooperation between production scheduling and inventory control by showing them how such cooperation can enhance the extent to which each achieves its distinct objectives over the long run, he is engaging in attitudinal structuring. Attitudinal structuring is an interpersonal process designed to change attitudes and relationships among members of the buying center.

4. *Intra-organizational bargaining* is defined in the Walton-McKerzie model as "the system of activities that brings the expectations of principals into alignment with those of the chief negotiator." [15] Implicit in this definition is the existence of another member of the organization who plays the role of another negotiator. In the purchasing situation, intra-organizational bargaining is seen in the attempts of the purchasing agent to achieve consensus among the members of his organization to a viewpoint which he can represent in his dealings with potential suppliers. In other words, intra-organizational bargaining involves the search for a compromise among the distinct interests of members of the buying center for the purpose of defining the terms on which they will do business with suppliers.

[14] Richard E. Walton and Robert B. McKerzie, *A Behavioral Theory of Labor Negotiations* (New York: McGraw-Hill Book Company, Inc., 1965), 4–6.

[15] *Ibid.*, 5.

The social negotiations model attempts to analyze and structure essentially the same kinds of interactions and relationships as the lateral relationships model, but it emphasizes different aspects of the relationship between buyers and others. Instead of placing the emphasis upon the buyer's desire for increased organizational status and authority, the social negotiations model emphasizes the negotiative aspects of the buyer's responsibilities and seems more directly related to the work he must perform. Distributive and integrative bargaining are necessary to obtain a workable definition of the buying problem and an operational set of product specifications and delivery requirements. Attitudinal structuring and intra-organizational bargaining are necessary to define a set of working relationships that permit the buyer to represent the organization unambiguously in his dealings with vendors. He must present a united front, and this requires a spirit of cooperation among members of the buying center. Thus, the model of social negotiations is a useful way for thinking about the purchasing agent or buyer as the key decision-maker in the organizational buying process.

The Buying Committee

The buying committee is a special case of interpersonal influences in organizational buying in which several members of the organization simultaneously listen to presentations by representatives of potential suppliers and participate in what may be called a group decision-making process. Buying committees are used where the judgments of several organizational members are felt necessary to evaluate alternative buying actions. They are commonly found in large retailing organizations, especially in the grocery field, where the decision is essentially a go/no-go decision as to whether to stock a particular product and involves judgments about consumer acceptance. In this case, the principal objective of the buying committee is to obtain an assortment of merchandise to be offered in the retail outlet; it is not concerned with the buying decision process as defined earlier, where there are certain organizational problems to be solved by buying action.

Buying committees, whether a regular part of the purchasing function or on an *ad hoc* basis (such as in the case of the purchase of a new computer), are intended to be an efficient way of making buying decisions. Buying committees are often found in organizations where several distinct viewpoints are represented in the buying situation and need to be taken into consideration in evaluating buying alternatives.

Being a special case of group decision making and behavior, buying committees are likely to encounter four types of problems: [16]

1. *Problems of Objectives.* Buying committees, being composed of individuals representing various organizational groups, face three possible levels of conflict of objec-

[16] The following discussion is based primarily on Harold J. Leavitt, *Managerial Psychology*, 2nd ed. (Chicago: The University of Chicago Press, 1964), 252–67.

tives: (a) defining and agreeing on the objectives of the committee—the committee must decide whether it should select a vendor for supplying a given item, set the criteria for evaluating alternative vendors, or engage in the decision whether or not such an item is needed at all; (b) explicating and solving the conflicting objectives of the various departments represented, and the conflict between the departmental objectives and the committee's objectives; (c) determining the individual objectives and their congruency with the departments' and the committee's objectives.

2. *Problems of Personnel.* The second source of difficulty for a committee's activities centers in the personalities of the participants. Such personality problems may involve such characteristics of the committee members as their talkativeness, shyness, defensiveness, friendliness, argumentativeness, and especially the leader's personality, his dominance or submissiveness, his leadership pattern, his desire to be liked, and so on.

3. *Problems of Navigation and Leadership.* Committees can get so involved in their activities and content matters that they may lose direction. It is one of the functions of the committee's leadership to provide the required direction. In addition, the leadership should open and maintain communication among the committee members and help resolve the various problems confronting the operation of the comimttee.

4. *Problems of Decision Making.* Even if one assumes that the specific decisions a buying committee has to make can be made more efficiently by a group than by an individual, there will still remain some decision-making issues, such as the need for unanimity versus the majority rule, specificity versus general decisions, and so forth.

Given that the performance of a buying committee may be influenced by any of these problems, an understanding of the committee and its various problems is obviously critical to those companies selling in markets where buying committees are common. Committees can present a real problem for the selling company if, for example, members of the committee are not in agreement about the criteria to be used in evaluating alternative sources of supply. Yet seven when there is no buying committee and the purchasing agent has the final buying authority, a disagreement on criteria between him and some other influencers may cause the selling company considerable problems. One should therefore view buying committees as a special case of interpersonal influences in organizational buying, and should attempt to understand the operating forces within the committee (or buying center), to identify the key decision-makers and influencers in each of the stages of the buying process (not all members of the committee have the same influence), and to influence them.

Summary

Interpersonal influences in the organizational buying decision process reflect the many different viewpoints of those organizational members who perceive that buying decisions are important to their performance within the organization. Users, influencers, deciders, buyers, and gatekeepers interact to determine the outcome of the decision. Although the buyer has formal authority for the buying decision, his actual influence on the outcome of the decision process may be significantly reduced as the result of the influence of others at earlier stages of the buying process which defines the constraints on the feasible set of buying actions.

Buyers who are ambitious and wish to extend the scope of their influence will adopt certain tactics and engage in bargaining activities in an attempt to become more influential at earlier stages of the buying process. These tactics or bargaining strategies define the nature of the buyer's relationships with others of equal organizational status and structure the social situation that the potential supplier must face in dealing with the buying organization. An understanding of the nature of interpersonal relationships in the buying organization is an important basis for the development of marketing strategy.

7

INDIVIDUAL BEHAVIOR AND ORGANIZATIONAL BUYING

In the final analysis, all organizational buying behavior is individual behavior. The individual may be acting on behalf of others, may be influenced by purposes beyond his own, and may interact with others, but organizational behavior is, after all, the behavior of individuals in an organizational context. Only the person can think, feel, and act although each aspect of individual behavior may be significantly influenced by the people, tasks, structure, and technology of the organization.

At the heart of the organizational buying process, then, is the individual —a person both influencing and influenced by the other persons around him and by the organization and its various subsystems. Imbedded within these various influences (which, as we have seen, have both task and non-task dimensions), the individual makes his unique contribution to the workings of the organization. To understand organizational buying behavior we need to understand also the behavior of the organizational buyer as an *individual*.

In some respects, the individual buyer (or decider, or influencer) within the organization is similar to the individual consumer or household purchaser. Certainly, the same basic mental processes—motivation, cognition, and learning—are basic psychological processes that must occur in all buying behavior.

In other respects, the buying behavior of individuals within the context of the organization is different from all other forms of buying behavior. As a member of the organization, the individual's behavior is influenced by the extent to which he accepts the goals of the organization as his personal objectives. He is also influenced by organizational members and structure, as we have seen in Chapters 5 and 6. Furthermore the organizational buyer is in a unique position by virtue of the information structure available to him within and through the organization. He may be exposed to a particular variety of information sources only because he is a member of that buying organization.

With appropriate adjustments for the unique aspects of individual behavior in an organization context, we can apply several important concepts and research findings about individual behavior to our analysis of the organizational buying process. Psychology is the study of individual behavior, and we can turn to psychology for insights into the behavior of the organizational buyer.

It is not our purpose to review all of the relevant literature on individual behavior as it might pertain to organizational buying behavior. Rather, our purpose is to suggest a framework for thinking about individual behavior within the context of the organizational buying process. Within this framework, specific study results pertaining to organizational buying can be examined.

A Model of Individual Buying Behavior

Although there is no universal agreement about the best way to describe human behavior, there does seem to be some consensus that individual behavior is a function of three factors: (1) the person's personality, motivation, cognitive structure, and learning (habit and attitude formation) process; (2) his interaction with the environmental situation; and (3) his preference structure and decision model.

The specific interrelationships among these factors, and especially among the various "basic psychological processes" of motivation, cognition, and learning, are to a large extent unknown. Both behavioral scientists and marketing scholars have speculated on the process that takes place within the so-called "black box" that represents the individual's system of processing inputs to produce behavior.[1] However, most of these attempts have not been empirically verified. It is thus suggested that an operational model of individual buying behavior should focus on a central measurable process which can explain and predict subsequent behavior. In the context of organizational buying it is postulated that this central process is the person's preference structure and decision model.

Focusing on the individual's preference structure and decision model as the central explanatory and predictive variable of buyer behavior has considerable implications for organizational buying research inasmuch as it allows one to focus on this operationally measured variable and to avoid the need to measure a large number of abstract constructs (such as motivation and cognition) and to assess their interrelationships. This does not imply, however, that the other determinants of individual behavior should be ignored. On the contrary, understanding of these constructs may provide useful insight into the individual's behavior and suggest guidelines for the design of appropriate marketing strategies.

[1] An example of a psychologist's view is Edward C. Tulman, "A Psychological Model" in Talcott Parsons and Edward A. Shils, eds., *Toward a General Theory of Action* (Cambridge, Mass.: Harvard University Press, 1951). For a marketing scholar's attempt to explain buyer behavior, see John A. Howard and Jagdish N. Sheth, *The Theory of Buyer Behavior* (New York: John Wiley & Sons, Inc., 1969).

A simplified overview of individual behavior is summarized in Figure 7–1. The following discussion of individual determinants of organizational

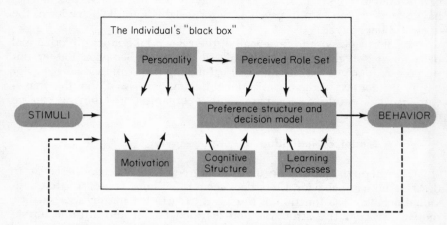

FIGURE 7–1.   A Simplified Model of Individual Behavior

buying behavior is divided into two parts. First, the discussion centers on the relevance of personality, role set, motivation, cognition, and learning to the understanding of buyer's behavior. This is followed by a brief discussion of the nature and importance of the buyer's predispositions, preference structure, and decision model.

PERSONALITY

Personality—the dynamic organization within the individual of those psychological systems that determine his characteristic behavior and thought [2] —whether considered a result of heredity, environment, or both, is one of the major determinants of the way an individual behaves and adjusts to his environment. Consequently, the way an individual carries out an organizational buying task will depend in part on his personality.

The degree to which a buyer tends, for example, to dominate and lead, or to yield and follow in his social relationships, to be an extrovert (dominated by external and social reality) or an introvert (approaching the world in terms of relevance to himself), to be authoritarian or not, may affect the relative strength of his position in the buying center, as well as his relations to others. More fundamentally, a buyer's personality may affect the way he adjusts to the environmental, organizational, and interpersonal climate within which he operates and the way he carries out the

[2] Gordon W. Allport, *Pattern and Growth in Personality* (New York: Holt, Rinehart & Winston, Inc., 1961).

buying task. Although personality conceptually seems to be a key determinant of organizational buying behavior, there is only one study which explores directly the link between the personality of organizational buyers and their behavior. In this study Wilson found that a purchasing agent's need for certainty and to some extent his degree of generalized self-confidence are good predictors of his decision-making style, whereas his need to achieve is not.[3] It is reasonable to assume that knowledge of the personality traits of members of a buying center may provide a marketer with useful guidelines for designing his marketing strategies. Questions remain, however, as to which specific personality measures to use and whether it is at all possible for a marketer to assess the personality characteristics of organizational buyers.

In general, utilizable personality measures can be classified into three major categories: (1) comprehensive personality measures; (2) socially oriented personality measures; and (3) intraperson-oriented personality measures.

Comprehensive Personality Measures. Of the all encompassing personality inventories, the Edwards Personality Preference Schedule (EPPS) has been the most commonly used in marketing studies concerning household consumers.[4] This test appraises the motivational dispositions of the respondents along the following dimensions: achievement, deference, order, exhibition, autonomy, affiliation, intraception, succorance, dominance, abasement, nurturance, change, endurance, heterosexuality, and aggression. Yet, the ability of the EPPS to predict and explain consumer buying behavior is quite limited,[5] and similar conclusions can be reached with regard to most other comprehensive personality tests. The usefulness of these tests in assessing the personality of organizational buyers is therefore quite doubtful. One possible exception is, however, tests designed to measure a person's self concept. Both behavioral scientists and marketing scholars have recognized the importance of the concept of "self"—a person's perception of himself—in determining one's behavior. Combs and Snygg in recognizing the broad scope of a person's evaluations, perceptions, and definitions of self, noted that whether we have come to think of ourselves as being competent or incompetent, attractive or repulsive, honest or dishonest, has a tremendous effect on our behavior in different situations.[6]

A number of consumer behavior studies have revealed a link between a person's self concept and his purchase behavior. A similar link may be hypothesized to exist in organizational buying situations, so that the buyer's

[3] David T. Wilson, "An Exploratory Study of the Effects of Personality and Problem Elements upon Purchasing Agent Decision Styles." Unpublished Ph.D. Dissertation, University of Western Ontario, London, Ontario, Canada, April 1970.

[4] A. Edwards, *Edwards Personal Preference Schedule Manual*, revised ed. (New York: Psychological Corporation, 1955).

[5] See, for example, William F. Massy, Ronald E. Frank, and T. M. Lodahl, *Purchasing Behavior and Personal Attributes* (Philadelphia: University of Pennsylvania Press, 1968).

[6] A. W. Combs and D. Snygg, *Individual Behavior*, rev. ed. (New York: Harper & Row, Publishers, Inc., 1959), 44–45 and 122–64.

concept of himself and his organization may affect his preference among various suppliers.

Socially Oriented Personality Measures. Aside from the comprehensive personality measures that attempt to assess the totality of one's personality, there are a number of measures designed to measure a person's social orientation. For example, Reisman's concept of social character, which distinguishes between inner-, other-, and tradition-oriented people, may prove a useful way of looking at organizational buyers.[7] Thus it can be hypothesized that an "other-directed" buyer will place more weight in his buying decisions on the opinions of others than will an "inner-directed" buyer. Furthermore, on the basis of various consumer behavior studies it can be hypothesized that a person's susceptibility to social influence as measured by the social character scales may affect his communication behavior.[8]

Intraperson-oriented Personality Measures. Although all personality traits have some effect on a person's relations with others, some of the personality traits can be classified as intrapersonal on the basis of their primary orientation. Measures of these traits are again quite varied and include scales for gauging dominant motivational traits emphasizing a master ego integrative motive related to one's self. Among the intraperson-oriented personality theories some of the better known are McClelland's "achievement motive," Allport's "creative becoming," and of course Rogers and Maslow's "self-actualization" motive.[9] Because self-actualization was at the top of his hierarchy of needs, Maslow investigated the characteristics of the self-actualized person and found fifteen major characteristics, such as spontaneity, problem centering, need for privacy, independence of culture and environment, democratic character structure, discrimination between means and ends, and creativeness.

Conceptually, then, assessing the degree of a buyer's self actualization or his score on a dominant trait such as venturesomeness (willingness to take risks) may provide a marketer with useful insight into the determinants of the buyer's decisions.

ROLE SET

The organization member is motivated by a complex combination of personal and organizational objectives. Although financial gain, ego-

[7] David Reisman, Nathan Glazer, R. Denney, *The Lonely Crowd: A Study of the Changing American Character* (New Haven: Yale University Press, 1961).

[8] Harold H. Kassarjian, "Social Character and Differential Preference for Mass Communication," *Journal of Marketing Research,* II (May 1965), 146–53.

[9] David C. McClelland, J. W. Atkinson, R. A. Clark, E. L. Lowell, *The Achievement Motive* (New York: Appleton-Century-Crofts, 1955); G. W. Allport, *Becoming: Basic Considerations for a Psychology of Personality* (New Haven: Yale University Press, 1955); C. R. Rogers, *Client-Centered Therapy* (Boston: Houghton-Mifflin, 1951); and A. H. Maslow, *Motivation and Personality* (New York: Harper and Row, 1954).

enhancement, esteem, and individual achievement are personal needs, their satisfaction depends significantly upon the extent to which the individual can help the organization to achieve its objectives. On the one hand, the individual implicitly has made the judgment (in his decision to be employed by a particular organization) that he can most effectively achieve his personal objectives in this form of employment. On the other hand, the organization's evaluation of his performance in his position will be a major determinant of the extent to which he accomplishes his individual goals. The evaluation of his performance will reflect the extent to which he has helped the organization successfully achieve its purpose.

The *role* of the individual within the organization is an important determinant of his behavior in the buying situation. A *role* is a social position occupied by an individual, including the goals of that position and the behavioral repertoire appropriate to it and to the attainment of those goals. The concept of role is complex and can be thought of as including three distinct components:

1. the *prescribed* role consisting of the expectations that exist in the social world for the behavior of persons occupying a position, especially regarding behavior toward persons in other positions;

2. the *subjective* role consisting of the expectations that a person has for his own behavior in reference to persons in other positions; and

3. the *enacted* role consisting of the actual behavior of the individual when he interacts with persons in other positions.[10]

An important feature of this definition of role is the emphasis it places upon the expectations of the "other person" and the individual's interpretation of those expectations as a basis for behavior. How an individual views his role (and he will have many roles) is likely to be affected in an important way by his choice of which of several relevant "other persons" he will interact with. For example, in the role of purchasing agent an individual is likely to have markedly different enacted roles in interacting with a salesman, a superior, subordinates (buyers), peers (in production or engineering, for example), or other purchasing agents. The purchasing agent therefore may have several concepts of his role, which vary with the persons with whom he is interacting. The term *role set* has been proposed to refer to "the complement of role relationships that persons have by virtue of occupying a particular social status."[11]

Thus the purchasing agent will be significantly influenced in his behavior by the expectations for his behavior (the prescribed role) which he attributes to relevant other persons. To the extent that he is predominantly "other-directed" and values their friendship, esteem, and approval, or to

[10] Morton Deutsch and Robert M. Krauss, *Theories in Social Psychology* (New York: Basic Books, Inc., 1965), 175.

[11] Robert Merton, *Social Theory and Social Structure*, rev. ed. (New York: The Free Press, 1957), p. 369, quoted in Deutsch and Krauss, *op. cit.*, 176.

the extent that he perceives that their evaluations of his performance will influence the gains he will derive from his job, he will attempt through his behavior to meet these expectations—i.e., to please these other people. The role set thus becomes an important source of goals for the individual as he attempts to achieve his personal objectives. In this way the individual's motives are related to his organizational position in a complex fashion as expressed by the concept of role set.

MOTIVATION

"Motivation" is a general term used to describe an individual's inner strivings that provide the impetus for his behavior. Terms such as wishes, desires, needs, goals, and the like are all synonyms for "motive."

Motivation implies the existence of an objective or goal object that can satisfy the need or needs that motivate behavior. Some act, event, or object will reduce the tension that the individual experiences either internally or in his perception of the environment. The individual seeking to satisfy his achievement needs may search his environment for opportunities for accomplishment and will remain satisfied in his job only so long as the challenge offered by it is at a level consistent with his felt need for individual accomplishment and his level of aspiration.

This consideration indicates the dynamic nature of motivation. Following March and Simon's model of adaptive motivated behavior, the following series of propositions can be stated: [12]

1. The lower the satisfaction of the organism, the more search for alternative programs it will undertake;
2. The more search, the higher the expected value of reward;
3. The higher the expected value of reward, the higher the expected satisfaction;
4. The higher the expected satisfaction, the higher the level of aspiration of the organism;
5. The higher the level of aspiration, the lower the satisfaction.

Seldom is behavior motivated by a single or simple motive. Most behavior is caused by complex combinations of motives at various levels of intensity. Being no exception the organizational buyer's behavior results from a complex combination of both task- and nontask-related motives, among other factors.

Task-Related Motives. Task-related variables were defined earlier in this volume as those variables relating specifically to the problem to be solved by buying action. In Chapter 2 the "lowest total cost" model of buying behavior saw the purpose of the buying task as buying the "right"

---

[12] James G. March and Herbert A. Simon, *Organizations* (New York: John Wiley & Sons, Inc., 1958).

quality at the "right" price from the "right" source at the "right" time. Although this is an oversimplified view of buying behavior, it helps to define the important task variables of product quality, price, service, and delivery. These buying variables determine the extent to which the buying action taken is consistent with the goals of the organization and the organization problem to be solved by the buying action. The definition is nearly tautological, however, inasmuch as it leaves unanswered the more important question of what is meant by "right," except for noting that "right" means optimum in terms of organizational objectives.

Because of identification with the goals of the organization, as well as a direct calculation that personal success depends upon successful job performance, the organizational buyer may be motivated by a desire to buy the most appropriate product or service for the need at hand and to do so at the lowest available price consistent with the organization's needs for service and delivery. To the extent that the buyer views his own welfare as consistent with that of the organization and to the extent that he identifies with the role of professional buyer, he will experience pride and a sense of achievement whenever he makes a "good buy" as defined by these or any other acceptable criteria.

Because the various relevant other persons whose expectations help the individual define his role set have different goals, they are likely to have different criteria in mind for judging the individual's performance. For example, a financial officer of the organization may be concerned primarily with the impact of the purchasing decision on the organization's cash position whereas a maintenance foreman may be concerned about the frequency of repairs. In these cases of potential conflict, the individual decision-maker may have to decide which set of criteria is most important. In making such judgments he may follow the behavior specified by a task-centered "reward-balance" model and consider several task factors, such as the extent to which he perceives each set of expectations as "legitimate."

Nontask-Related Motives. Nontask-related motives are those which are not directly related to the solution to the problem that created the buying situation, although they may be indirectly related to it. In other words, there is no necessary conflict between task and nontask variables, and in fact the pursuit of nontask objectives may be completely consistent with the attainment of task objectives.

Organizational members are motivated by several nontask variables, including the desire for promotion, salary raises, increased job security, and more interesting job assignments. It is possible to identify two important classes of nontask motives: achievement motives and risk-reduction motives, which will be discussed separately although they are interrelated.

Achievement motives are those concerned with personal advancement and recognition. In a study of purchasing agents, Duncan found that "recognition of accomplishment through advancement" was the most frequently cited factor stimulating the purchasing agent to improved performance. Sixty percent of his respondents gave this reason, followed by 20 percent who cited the fact that their recommendations would be accepted by top management and 5.7 percent who cited an increase in salary.[13] Research by Strauss indicated that purchasing agents were motivated by a desire to enhance their status and position within the organization.[14]

The individual is also motivated by a desire to reduce uncertainty. For the organizational buyer, three kinds of uncertainty can be significant. First, the organizational buyer may be uncertain about the alternative courses of buying action available to him; He can never be sure that he has identified *all* possible buying alternatives. Second, he may be uncertain about the outcomes of the identified courses of action; for example, factors such as vendor performance or product quality are difficult to predict in the absence of previous experience. Third, the organizational buyer may be uncertain about the manner in which relevant other persons will react to his buying decisions, either because he is uncertain about their goals or because he is uncertain about how rewards will accompany successful (or unsuccessful) goal accomplishment. Stated differently, he may be uncertain about both role expectations and reward structures. The individual will be motivated by a desire to reduce these three kinds of uncertainty.

COGNITION

Cognition is the process by which the individual receives information from the environment and interprets it. Cognition includes both sensation and perception. Sensation is the apprehension of stimuli from the environment, a response of the sense organs to physical changes in the environment and the experienced results of that process. Perception is the more complex process by which the individual selects and interprets such stimuli and organizes them into a coherent picture of the world.[15] Cognition includes all those mental processes that are involved in the development of this "organized picture of the world"—including perception, thinking, and memory—and which direct overt behavior toward the satisfaction of needs and the accomplishment of personal objectives.[16] The mental processes that comprise a person's cognitive structure can be divided into two sets: the first includes the three *selective processes* of selective attention, selective perception, and selective retention which are discussed next; the second is comprised primarily of the person's decision process and is discussed in this chapter in the section on preference structure and decision models.

[13] Delbert J. Duncan, *Some Basic Determinants of Behavior in Industrial Purchasing*, Reprint No. 7, Research Program in Marketing, Graduate School of Business Administration, Institute of Business and Economic Research, University of California (Berkeley), 1965, 5.

[14] George Strauss, "Tactics of Lateral Relationship," *Administrative Science Quarterly*, VII (September 1962), 161–86.

[15] Bernard Berelson and Gary A. Steiner, *Human Behavior: An Inventory of Scientific Findings* (New York: Harcourt Brace Jovanovich, Inc., 1964), 88.

[16] Rom J. Markin, *The Psychology of Consumer Behavior* (Englewood Cliffs, N.J.: Prentice-Hall, Inc., 1969), 84.

Selective Attention.   The individual buyer actively participates in the communication process by selecting, from all those messages to which he is exposed, those which he will actually take notice of. Not all physical stimuli in the environment have an equal impact on the individual. Out of all those messages about products and vendors to which he is exposed, from salesmen, direct mail, advertising, sales promotions, and so on, the organizational buyer will actually pay attention to a relatively small number—those which are most favorable to his existing predispositions and which otherwise can penetrate the barrier of sensation.

Through his information-processing habits the individual selects the messages to which he will be exposed. The buyer will decide whether or not to talk with a particular salesman; he will turn to certain published information sources and avoid others; he will subscribe to certain trade journals and newspapers and therefore create at least the possibility of his being reached through these media while excluding the possibility of being reached through other media. He also will develop habits for interacting with other people within his organization and in other organizations and for depending upon them for certain kinds of information.

From all those messages to which he is exposed and which actually impinge upon his senses, the individual will select those to which he will pay attention. Selective exposure is followed by selective attention, the filtering of all stimuli to admit into the individual's cognition only certain stimuli. Selective attention occurs in a manner consistent with the buyer's predispositions and preferences. The organizational buyer will not pay attention to all of the advertisements in the trade magazines that he reads nor will he use all of the catalogs available to him.

Selective Perception.   Perception is the assigning of meaning to stimuli from the environment. In this respect, the cognitive structure provides categories of meaning through which new information is processed and from which it takes on meaning. Perception is selective in that the individual actively assigns meaning to stimuli, reflecting his subjective interpretation of them.

In responding to communication, the individual will modify the message to make it more consistent with his cognitive structure and predispositions. The individual may distort the message by "sharpening" it (i.e., adding elements to it to make it consistent with predispositions) or by "leveling" it (subtracting elements). In either case, the resulting message may not be that intended by the source.

Selective perception is one of the best known generalizations of psychology based upon many, many studies. In organizational buying, selective perception becomes an important consideration in several respects. An individual's predispositions toward a company (or that company's image in the mind of that buyer) can significantly influence his response to a sales presentation by that company's salesman.

Selective Retention.   The organizational buyer will store in his memory those pieces of information and those evaluations that are most consistent with predispositions and favorable to them. It is well known that individuals are more likely to remember pleasurable experiences and to forget unpleasant ones. This is an important defense mechanism that helps preserve emotional stability.

If the organizational buyer was actively seeking new information, he is likely to remember it once obtained. If his acquisition of the information was just happenstance, however, he is less likely to remember it. In other words, the state of the individual's motives is an important determinant of selective retention.

There are often long time lags between marketing stimuli and buying responses. Organizational buying is complex and takes time. Many organizational marketing strategies are designed to lead to a slow change of predispositions by creating awareness of, and favorable attitudes toward, the company and its products. The success of this "goodwill building" kind of marketing strategy depends upon the ability of the potential customer to retain these message effects over time. The fact of selective retention suggests that marketing communications not only should provide information, but also should motivate the potential buyer in order to provide an incentive to retain the effects of the communication until action is possible.

Selective attention, perception, and retention are basic facts about individual cognitive processes that affect the individual's buying response to marketing efforts. Information about potential vendors and their products will be filtered through the buyer's cognitive structure and will be interpreted in the light of the buyer's predispositions and preference structure.

LEARNING

The foregoing comments on the selective processes have suggested why organizational buyers often favor existing suppliers and maintenance of the *status quo*. Having found one or more sources of supply that permit acceptable solutions to the buying problem, the organizational buyer may be reluctant to incur the risk inherent in trying other courses of action. Only when the level of goal attainment becomes unsatisfactory will the organizational buyer consider other alternatives and shift from a straight rebuy to a modified rebuy situation. The buyer will consider additional alternatives either when he raises his goals (perhaps stimulated by a prospective vendor's marketing effort), when he perceives change in any of the relevant variables affecting the buying decisions, or when he feels that the performance of present products and vendors has become unsatisfactory.

Learning is the process by which behavior is influenced by previous behavior in similar situations. If behavior is successful in moving the individual toward an objective, the attainment of the goal will reinforce the behavior. If behavior is consistently successful, reinforced learning will occur to the point where the behavior becomes "habitual," which is to say that the amount of cognitive extensive decision-making activity has decreased to the point at which the response to a stimulus becomes virtually automatic.

Much organizational buying is habitual behavior. Because of the many demands upon the organizational buyer's time, and because of the many goods and services purchased by the typical organization, there is a real tendency for the "squeaky wheel to get the grease." Acceptable-level buying solutions tend to be repeated, making organizational buying more or less routine. Because of loyalty to existing suppliers and a reluctance to consider new alternatives, there is a tendency, when new needs arise, to favor known suppliers and those with whom the organization is regularly doing business.

Learning occurs in information-handling as well as in buying action. The organization buyer learns to depend upon certain information sources and these then define the set of buying stimuli to which that buyer will be exposed under normal circumstances. "In" suppliers may be favored not only because of their previous performance in providing products and services but also because they have become trusted and valuable sources of information about other products as needs have arisen. There is a well known tendency for problem-solvers, especially in an organizational context, to search for solutions to problems in an area which has previously been the source of helpful information.

Thus dependence on learned responses is by no means "irrational," however. The buyer may have learned through repeated experience that this one course of action is clearly the best. Risk reduction motives will lead him to not consider new alternatives because of perceived high costs of being wrong.

Preference Structure and Decision Models

We have now considered the organizational buyer's personality and perceived role set, and the three basic psychological processes of motivation, cognition, and learning. These individual characteristics and mental processes interact to produce the buyer's predispositions, preference structure, and decision models. These three constructs can be thought of as intervening variables through which all other determinants of organizational buying behavior influence the individual's decision making.

PREDISPOSITIONS AND PREFERENCES

Predispositions and preferences both can be defined as tendencies to act in a particular way toward a particular object in the environment. They summarize the social and psychosocial state of the individual at a point in time in response to any stimulus. Predispositions and preferences reflect the individual's information, interests, attitudes, personality characteristics, group affiliations, organizational climate, or anything that characterizes him and may affect his response to a marketing stimulus. They include both affective and evaluative factors that incline him to respond either positively or negatively toward a stimulus. Predispositions and preferences are developed and modified as a result of the individual's interaction with his environment; they are both the result of experience and filters through which the experience is interpreted.

As a result of his previous experiences and his interactions with his colleagues, the organizational buyer develops a set of predispositions and preferences toward potential suppliers and their products. These predispositions and preferences can be defined in a variety of ways; they may reflect the buyer's awareness of these vendors and brands, his attitudes toward them, his previous experience with them, or the strength of his convictions concerning them.

DECISION MODELS

The main function of organizational buyers is to make appropriate buying decisions concerning what to buy, when, where, and how to buy, and who should make the purchase decisions and actions. An organizational buyer can utilize a variety of decision models. In general there are two types of possible models—dominant dimension models and multiattribute models. Of the dominant dimension models we will discuss in considerable detail the perceived risk model, which has a number of important implications for organizational marketing. Then we will discuss briefly an attempt to identify the "decision style" of organizational buyers.

The final section of this chapter is devoted to a short review of alternative multiattribute models that can be utilized by a buyer in making organizational buying decisions.

THE PERCEIVED RISK MODEL

In striving to attain personal goals and to satisfy personal needs, including the need for individual achievement and for reducing the amount of perceived risk, the organizational buyer adopts several problem-solving strategies. The perceived risk model, originally proposed by Bauer [17] and subsequently elaborated by Cox and others,[18] provides a useful framework within which to consider organizational buying behavior from the viewpoint of the individual. Although this is certainly not the only useful model of individual buying behavior of interest to students of organizational buying, it is the one most consistent with a view of organizational buying as "problem-solving" behavior. The perceived risk model of individual decision making behavior is also attractive in our theory of organizational buying behavior because many of its propositions are consistent with the

[17] Raymond A. Bauer, "Consumer Behavior as Risk Taking," in R. S. Hancock, ed., *Dynamic Marketing for a Changing World* (Chicago: American Marketing Association, 1960), 389–98.

[18] Donald F. Cox, ed., *Risk Taking and Information Handling in Consumer Behavior* (Boston: Division of Research, Graduate School of Business Administration, Harvard University, 1967).

behavioral theory of the firm, introduced in Chapter 5 as a valuable tool for analyzing organizational influences. Understanding the nature and components of perceived risk allows one to make a meaningful analysis of the strategies that organizational buyers adopt for reducing perceived risk to tolerable levels and, therefore, provides a framework within which to think about the requirements for effective marketing strategy.

COMPONENTS OF PERCEIVED RISK

Perceived risk is a function of the uncertainty which an individual has about the outcome of a given course of action and the consequences associated with alternative outcomes. The individual may be uncertain either about the goals that are relevant in the buying situation or about the extent to which a particular course of buying action will meet those goals. (These can be called goal *identification* uncertainty and goal/purchase *matching* uncertainty, respectively.)

Two types of consequences will be of importance as determinants of the amount of risk perceived by the organizational buyer in a given buying situation. First, uncertainty about the *performance* of certain products and vendors will be significant determinants of perceived risk. Second, the individual may be concerned about the reactions of other people to his decisions, the *psychosocial* consequences of his actions.

The importance of the consequences resulting from a given buying action will increase as a function of the importance of the goals being pursued and as a function of the amount of time, money, effort, and "psychosocial" investment involved in the buying decision. Obviously, a decision to buy a computer is more important than a decision to buy a delivery truck because of the amount of money involved. On the other hand, a firm with the goal of technical superiority in its products may see considerably more risk in its purchase of even relatively inexpensive component parts and subassemblies than in the purchase of major pieces of equipment.

STRATEGIES FOR REDUCING RISK

The formal definition of perceived risk identifies the major strategies available to the organizational buyer for reducing perceived risk. Given that perceived risk is a product of uncertainty and its consequences, it follows that perceived risk can be reduced either by reducing the uncertainty or by reducing the importance of the consequences. It further follows that the importance of the consequences can be reduced either by lowering the goals or by reducing the amount of investment (financial and/or psychosocial) in the buying decision.

Information collection and processing strategies, which reduce uncertainty, are a major class of risk-reducing behavior. In general, information about products and vendors reduces the amount of perceived risk by narrowing the range of expected outcomes. It reduces variance in the distribution of expected performance.

Just as information about product and vendor characteristics helps to reduce perceived performance risk, so information can be gathered to evaluate and reduce psychosocial risk. Discreet inquiries may reveal more clearly the expectations of other decision influencers within the organization. Superiors may be induced to be more explicit concerning goals and reward structures. The criteria being used to evaluate the organizational buyer may be made clearer. Information search and analysis are common strategies for reducing both performance and psychosocial risk because they help to clarify goals and to assess the ability of alternative courses of action to achieve those goals.

Another set of strategies for reducing perceived risk are goal reduction strategies. Goal level is a determinant of the amount of perceived risk. If the organizational buyer sets very tight product specifications, the chances are increased that a particular offering will not meet them. Both product performance risk and vendor selection risk increase as specifications become tighter.

The higher the level of personal goals the harder they are to meet, and frustration in goal attainment will lead eventually to goal reduction. Over time, the organizational buyer whose desire for advancement and promotion is not satisfied will reduce his desire for these rewards and will emphasize other needs, such as those for security or self-esteem. Every organization has members who want to "play it safe" and who avoid taking normal risks in pursuit of organizational objectives. Instead, they place greater emphasis on a higher probability of attaining a less desired but still acceptable outcome. They are risk-avoiders and have reduced their goals.

Goal reduction is also a likely strategy for reducing perceived risk where initial search fails to identify sufficient numbers of product/vendor offerings within the feasible set. A loosening of specifications and selection criteria can be seen as a goal-reducing strategy.

Loyalty to particular brands, vendors, and products is a risk-reducing strategy that maintains goals at an acceptable level. Instead of striving to do better, thereby increasing the risk of doing more poorly, the loyal buyer chooses the greater certainty afforded by a merely acceptable outcome. He implicitly says that the present level of goal attainment is adequate and routine reorder procedures are established. Loyalty also reduces perceived risk by reducing the amount of time and money invested in the search for new alternatives. Loyalty to a vendor or brand may also reflect a perception (based on previous experience) that there are few alternative sources offering better quality or service, so that the expected value of additional search is small.

A final set of strategies for reducing perceived risk are those that reduce the amount of investment. The organizational buyer may reduce either the amount of time and effort involved in search, the financial investment involved, or his own personal commitment to the buying situation. A decision to buy on a low-bid basis or to lease rather than buy is a form of investment-reducing strategy.

High perceived psychosocial risk can be reduced by decreasing the amount of personal involvement in the buying situation. The individual can adopt a "count-me-out" posture and refuse to accept responsibility for the outcome of the buying decision. Strauss' study found that among the tactics used by purchasing agents were those of ignoring requisitions from using departments and requiring the user to submit a written acceptance of responsibility for a buying action.[19]

The preceding paragraphs have identified four classes of strategies for reducing perceived risk: (1) information acquisition and processing; (2) goal reduction; (3) loyalty; and (4) investment reduction. Available evidence suggests that information handling is probably the most important strategy in terms of both frequency and impact. One of the major determinants of the ability of information to reduce risk is the credibility of the source of the communication.

SOURCE CREDIBILITY

The study of communication effects has found that the reputation of the source, or communicator, influences the audience response to the communication. Communicators of high credibility secure above average amounts of opinion change while those of low credibility secure below average opinion change. This is the so-called "source effect."

There are two dimensions to credibility: trustworthiness and expertise. Both dimensions relate to the ability of the communication to reduce the amount of uncertainty perceived by the receiver. Perceived trustworthiness increases the "confidence value" of the communication while perceived competence of the communicator increases the "predictive value."

Over time, the initial effects attributable to the credibility of the source disappear. When questioned at a later time, persons who were originally exposed to a high credibility source will show a decline in the amount of opinion change whereas those who were originally exposed to the low credibility source will show an increase. This is the so-called "sleeper effect," and it has been explained by the observation that persons tend to dissociate the message from its source as time passes. A good reputation heightens the initial impact of the message while the poor reputation of the source depresses the effect of the message.[20]

The existence of source and sleeper effects in the responses of organizational buyers to marketing communications has been confirmed by Levitt. He found that the reputation of the selling company was important in determining the reactions of industrial purchasing agents and industrial chemists to a salesman's presentation. He also found that the importance of source credibility increased as the amount of risk in the decision in-

19 Strauss, *op. cit.*

20 Carl I. Hovland, Irving L. Janis, and Harold H. Kelley, *Communication and Persuasion: Psychological Studies of Opinion Change* (New Haven: Yale University Press, 1951), esp. Chaps. 2 and 8.

creased. When buyers were asked whether they would actually buy a product (high-risk decision), as opposed to whether they would recommend it to others in the company for further evaluation (low-risk decision), they were likely to place more importance upon the reputation of the vendor. This greater impact of the well-known company's salesman diminished over time, however. Thus Levitt's research confirms the general finding of source and sleeper effects in the special case of industrial purchasing decisions.[21]

Perceived risk can be reduced if the credibility of the source is sufficient to reduce uncertainty about the outcome of alternative courses of action. The trustworthiness of the communicator as well as his expertise are important in determining the ability of the information to reduce the buyer's uncertainty. It is important to note that source credibility is a subjective characteristic ascribed to the source by the individual's perception of the communicator's competence and expertise. That is the reason why this phenomenon is discussed in this chapter dealing with individual behavior —it is a characteristic of communication sources *as perceived by the individual receiver.*

The perceived risk model contributes to our understanding of the impact of alternative sources of information upon buyer response. The communicator with highest credibility has the greatest probability of reducing perceived risk. Because of greater perceived trustworthiness, if not competence, personal friends and acquaintances in other organizations may be preferred as more credible sources because of their perceived "honesty" when compared with the salesmen and mass communications of potential vendors. On the other hand, the greater technical competence of the industrial salesman may give him greater credibility than a noncommercial source of information.

The perceived risk model provides an interesting framework within which to consider the individual buyer's motivations and their influence on his response to marketing effort. Since all buying action involves risk in one form or another because of the inherent uncertainties and the necessary investments of time, effort, and dollars, the perceived risk model is a useful way of analyzing organizational buying behavior. It is a model of individual behavior that emphasizes the buyer's motivations of achievement and risk-reduction and suggests some strategies which buyers are likely to use in their dealings with potential vendors.

BUYER'S DECISION STYLES

In an experiment designed to investigate the effect of uncertainty concerning the value of the outcome on the purchase decision, Wilson discovered three major decision styles—normative, conservative, and a mixed-mode

---

[21] Theodore Levitt, *Industrial Purchasing Behavior: A Study of Communications Effects* (Boston: Division of Research, Graduate School of Business Administration, Harvard University, 1965).

switcher.[22] The normative style was the one most consistent with an expected monetary value decision model. The conservative style took three forms: (1) avoidance of uncertainty surrounding the exact value of the outcome; (2) avoidance of uncertainty surrounding future states of nature; and (3) avoidance of large negative outcomes. The switcher style was characteristic of those subjects who switched from a normative to conservative pattern.

Purchasing agents with normative decision styles had the lowest need for certainty and did not generally overreact to the problem's elements. Subjects with a conservative decision style had a slightly higher need for certainty and were most sensitive to uncertainty surrounding future states of nature and large negative outcomes. Purchasing agents who switched from normative to conservative decision style had the highest need for certainty and appeared to be more sensitive to large negative outcome and less sensitive to uncertainty surrounding future states of nature than those with conservative decision styles.

Purchasing agents with different decision styles perceived the same supplier quite differently. The conservative decision style group perceived suppliers in general as more risky than the normative or switcher groups. If these observed differences in the behavior of purchasing agents with different styles will hold in other situations as well, it will be possible to segment organizations on the basis of the decision-makers' decision style. This is in turn may provide some guidelines for the design of appropriate marketing strategies. For example, organizational buyers with a normative decision style may respond more favorably to economic messages than buyers with a conservative decision style when they perceive high uncertainty and the decision involves a large financial outlay. On the other hand, the "conservative" buyer under these conditions may respond more favorably to messages aimed at reducing the negative outcome values and the uncertainty surrounding future states of nature and the outcome values.

MULTIATTRIBUTE DECISION MODELS

Whenever an organizational buyer decides which product to buy, which vendor to select or any other of the various buying decisions, he is faced with the problem of evaluating multiattribute alternatives. One vendor may be highly reliable on delivery but poor with respect to marketing services, while another may be merely adequate on both, and so on. In order to make buying decisions the organizational buyer must follow certain decision procedures.

Generally, a buyer may follow any one of a variety of composition functions—namely, conjunctive, disjunctive, lexicographic, or compensatory models, or any combination of them.[23] According to the conjunctive model,

[22] Wilson, op. cit.

[23] The following discussion is based primarily on Clyde H. Coombs, A Theory of Data (New York: John Wiley & Sons, Inc., 1964).

an individual will respond positively to a stimulus if and only if it meets certain minimum standards on *each* of the components of a complex set of criteria. In the organizational buying context a buyer utilizing this model will accept a supplier, for example, if and only if the supplier can satisfy the minimum requirement on each of a set of relevant attributes. This model is therefore implicit in any multiple cutoff criterion.

The disjunctive model requires a certain minimum on *any* of the relevant dimensions. For example, a buyer may accept a supplier under either of two conditions: if he can provide substantial cost savings or if he can provide an exceptionally good service.

The basic idea of a lexicographic model is that an ordering or hierarchy of importance exists among the relevant attributes. In the context of organizational buying, a buyer will prefer vendor A over B if vendor A is higher on the most important attribute, irrespective of the relative positions of the two vendors on the other attributes. Only if the two vendors are tied on the most important attribute will the buyer turn to the second most imporant attribute, and so on.

According to the compensatory model, a surplus on one component may substitute for a shortage on another. Following this model a buyer may select a supplier who is not very reliable in delivery but has exceptionally high quality products.

Organizational buyers in making their buying decisions may utilize, implicitly or explicitly, any of these models. Most of these decision models, and possibly others as well, can be identified and investigated empirically. Yet in the context of organizational buying behavior only one study explored the question of whether a linear compensatory model [24] can be used to determine the implicit importance coefficients which purchasing agents assign to vendors' performance characteristics in making selection decisions and to assess the relative importance of each performance characteristic.[25]

Understanding the buying decision-maker's decision-making process (problem identification → identification of alternatives → evaluation of alternatives → choice), and especially the model he uses for evaluating the alternatives, can serve as an operational surrogate for all the other determinants of the organizational buyer's behavior. This can therefore serve as a key input to the design of marketing strategies aimed at influencing the organizational buying decision process.

Summary

Organizational buying is carried out by organizational members (either as individuals or as members of a group) not in response to some physical reality but in response to the perceived reality defined by the individual's needs, goals, experience, and so on. The organization buyer's

[24] A model which assumes that the overall worth of a multiattribute alternative is equal to an additive combination of the partial worths.

[25] Yoram Wind, Paul E. Green, and Patrick J. Robinson, "The Determinants of Vendor Selection: The Evaluation Function Approach," *Journal of Purchasing*, IV (August 1968), 29–41.

personality, perceived role set, motivation, cognition, and learning are the basic psychological processes that affect his response to the definition of buying situations and marketing stimuli provided by potential vendors. This chapter has stressed the importance of understanding the buyer's psychological characteristics and especially his predispositions, preference structure, and decision model as the basis for making marketing strategy decisions and it has highlighted the individual determinants of buying behavior. Cultural, organizational, and social factors, as discussed in earlier chapters, are important influences on the individual and are reflected in his previous experiences, awareness of, and attitudes and preference toward particular vendors and products and his particular buying decision models.

We have now completed our discussion of the environmental, organizational, interpersonal, and individual factors that determine organizational buying behavior. What emerges from this is a view of the organizational buyer as a constrained decision-maker. Although based on the universally similar mental processes of motivation, cognition, and learning, the buyer's personality, perceived role set, preference structure, and decision model are uniquely individual and are influenced by the context of interpersonal and organization influences within which the individual is embedded. The organizational buyer is motivated by a complex combination of individual and organizational objectives and is dependent upon others for the satisfaction of these needs in several ways. These other people define the role expectations for the individual, they determine the payoffs he is to receive for his performance, they influence the definition of the goals to be pursued in the buying decision, and they provide information with which the individual attempts to evaluate risks and come to a decision.

Only rarely can the organizational buyer let purely personal considerations influence his buying decisions. In a situation where "all other things are equal" the individual may be able to apply strictly personal (nontask) criteria when making his final decision. In the unlikely event that two or more potential vendors offer products of comparable quality at a comparable price with comparable service, then the organizational buyer may be motivated by purely personal, nontask variables such as his personal preferences for dealing with a particular salesman, or some special favor or gift available from the supplier.

Once again in this chapter, as in earlier chapters, we see that both task and nontask variables must be considered in the analysis of organizational buying behavior. They interact in complex ways to determine the objectives for which the organizational buyer is striving and the criteria that will be used to evaluate alternative courses of buying action.

8

IMPLICATIONS FOR MARKETING STRATEGY

Marketing is a communication process. The marketing manager's objective is to influence buyers to behave in a manner consistent with the interests of his firm. It was the contribution of the marketing concept to recognize that, in a free enterprise economy, the buyer has more power than the seller in most market relationships.[1] Because the buyer typically has a wide range of alternative buying actions available to him, the seller who wants to influence a buyer must show how his product-service offering provides the best solution to the buyer's problem. The philosophy of the preceding chapters therefore has been a pragmatic one: effective marketing strategy for organizational markets requires accurate information about buyers as the basis for understanding and predicting their response to marketing effort. Data, which are uninterpreted facts, become information when relevant analytical concepts are applied to them by the decision-maker. Information about buyer behavior then helps the decision-maker reduce his uncertainty about alternative strategic actions and choose those most likely to produce buyer response consistent with company objectives.

The purpose of this book has been to develop a conceptual framework for the analysis of markets for those firms whose customers are formal organizations. In this chapter, the concepts developed in earlier chapters will be pulled together into an integrated framework and its implications for marketing strategy will be drawn.

An Integrated Framework

Several "partial" models of organizational buying behavior have been developed in earlier chapters. These models were concerned with

---

[1] For an alternative view, however, see John K. Galbraith, *The New Industrial State* (Boston: Houghton Mifflin Company, 1967).

subsets of the many variables and processes that are involved in buyer response to marketing action. It is now time to review these submodels and to integrate them into a consistent framework. This framework is based on integrating the organizational buying model developed in Chapter 3 (see Figure 3–1) with the various marketing decisions faced by firms whose customers are formal organizations.

In Chapter 1, a simple model of market response was introduced which saw the buyer as a "black box" that processed information from the seller's marketing actions and generated outputs in the form of buyer responses. Later in that chapter, throughout the book, and especially in Chapter 3, two important aspects of organizational buying behavior were recognized. First, organizational buying is not a single act. Rather, it is a decision process. Second, "the organizational buyer" is influenced by four sets of factors: individual, interpersonal, organizational, and environmental. These variables can be dichotomized as either "task-related" (related to the organizational buying problem as defined by organizational objectives) or "nontask-related" (not directly related to the buying problem).

Chapter 4 discussed six sets of environmental influences—physical, technological, economic, political, legal, and cultural—which affect the organizational buying decisions both directly and through a variety of institutions. Chapter 4 also considered the changing nature of the environment, ecological consequences of buying decisions, technological and environmental forecasting, diffusion of innovations among organizations, and subcultures among professional personnel in buying organizations.

In Chapter 5 several classes of organizational factors were defined and analyzed, including the organizational and buying tasks, structure (systems of communication, authority, status, rewards, and work flow), technology, and personnel. The chapter focused on the composition of the buying center and the effect of centralization and decentralization on the buying decisions. Finally, the chapter explored the behavioral theory of the firm and its applicability to organizational buying behavior.

Chapter 6 stressed the fact that "the organizational buyer" is not one but many individuals within the organization. It examined the various buying roles—users, influencers, buyers, deciders, and gatekeepers—within the buying center, and the nature of relationships among members of the buying center.

Chapter 7 focused on the individual in the buying situation and identified five psychological forces—personality, perceived role set, motivation, cognition, and learning—affecting the buyer's buying decision. The characteristics and quality of seller-provided information took on particular significance, in terms of the ability of this information to reduce perceived risk.

Although frequently presented as self-contained models, these various approaches and explanations of organizational buying behavior should be viewed as parts of the complex organizational buying behavior model presented in Figure 3–1. This suggests that the various partial models and explanations presented in this book are entirely consistent with one another and can be integrated into one conceptual framework.

Implicit in our model of the organizational buying process is an extremely important assertion: all organizational buying behavior is *individual* behavior. Organizations do not make decisions, individuals do. Individuals, acting in their organizational roles, commit the organization to buy. Organizations do not act. People act on behalf of the organization, motivated by the desire for rewards of income, status, and ego-satisfaction provided by the organization. Of course, interpersonal relationships within the organization, the organization itself (its structure, policies and procedures, communication patterns, reward systems, etc.), and the environment are crucial influences on the individual's motivation, information search, and choice at all stages of the decision process and in all buying roles.

The organizational buying model presents a framework for analyzing and understanding organizational buying behavior. This provides the marketing personnel of firms whose customers are organizational buyers with guidelines for collecting and analyzing the required marketing information. This information ideally should cover four major aspects of organizational buying:

1. The identity of the buying center;
2. The nature of the buying decision process;
3. The buying situation (new task versus modified rebuy versus straight rebuy);
4. The nature of the factors affecting the buying decisions—the environmental, organizational, interpersonal, and individual characteristics.

Knowing this information provides the marketing strategist with the necessary inputs to answer the following marketing questions:

1. Which market segment(s) should the firm pursue?
2. What should be the firm's marketing strategy concerning products, price, promotion (both personal and non-personal), and distribution?
3. How should the marketing function be managed? I.e., how should marketing operations be organized, planned, implemented and controlled?
4. What should be the marketing research activities of the firm?

An integrative model of organizational buying behavior, in order to be of value in the design of organizational marketing strategies, should incorporate both the marketing decisions and the organizational buying behavior information required for making them. Table 8–1 suggests the framework for such an integrative model.

Information Required by the Marketing Strategist

The integrated framework presented in Table 8–1 provides a convenient classification scheme for the variables and processes that must be understood by the marketing strategist. From the framework, it is possible

TABLE 8–1. An Integrative Model of Organizational Buying Behavior
as a Guideline for Marketing Decisions

Marketing Decisions	Information Required for Making Marketing Decisions							
	Identity of buying center	Nature of buying decision process	Buying situation	Nature of Factors Affecting Buying Decision			
				Environ- mental factors	Organi- zational factors	Inter- personal factors	Personal charac- teristics
1. Identify target market segments							
2. Determine market mix strategies							
a. Product strategy							
b. Price strategy							
c. Promotion strategy							
i. Impersonal communica- tion							
ii. Personal communica- tion							
d. Distribution strategy							
3. Management of organizational marketing							
a. Organizing							
b. Planning							
c. Controlling							
4. Marketing research							

to see that the marketer must understand, at the minimum, the composition of the buying center, the decision stages that characterize the buying decision process for his product or service, the buying situation, and the buyer's predispositions and preferences.

COMPOSITION OF THE BUYING CENTER

An efficient and effective marketing strategy for organizational buyers must be aimed at specific individuals who have authority and responsibility for buying decisions, not at some broad conception of the "organization," for individuals, not organizations, make organizational buying decisions. Whether the planner is a vice president of marketing, a sales manager, an advertising manager, or a sales representative, his strategic planning must be directed toward those members of the buying center who will influence and determine response to his marketing efforts. For the sales representative, this information must be specific to the particular organizations that are his assigned accounts; for the other planners, information about general tendencies for groups of accounts and for the total market may be more desirable.

It is useful to recall that the buying center is composed of all individuals who will influence the buying decision process, including users, buyers, deciders, influencers, and gatekeepers. Simply recognizing that there are multiple roles in the buying process can serve the purpose of reminding the strategist that he must identify those individuals who occupy these roles within the organization. In multiplant organizations, the problem of identifying the buying center can be very complex.

In addition to identifying the key buying personnel within the customer organization, it is also useful to understand their relative power and the relationships among them. A key question in virtually every buying organization is the extent to which the purchasing agent actually influences the decision process at each of the buying stages. While there is probably no case where the purchasing agent has either complete authority or no authority, there are tremendous variations among buying organizations in the power of the chief purchasing official. Treatises on organizational buying are unanimous in their warnings that the purchasing agent does not have sole responsibility, but the marketing practitioner who assumes that the purchasing manager has little or no authority is often operating on a false premise.

Information flows among members of the buying organization—who talks to whom—are likely to provide a reliable picture of the flow of influence through the stages of the decision process. It may be possible to reach some members of the buying organization only through other members of that organization.

There is no more important task in the planning of marketing strategy than identifying those individuals who share responsibility and authority for the buying decision. They become the target for all marketing effort.

NATURE OF THE BUYING DECISION PROCESS

All buying decisions begin with the identification of need and culminate in the selection of one or more suppliers. Each of the five stages of the decision process is likely to occur as a more or less distinct and identifiable phenomenon, although some stages may be repeated several times and the organizational buying process may "jump around" from one stage to the next. After the vendor has been chosen, a variety of decisions may be required to maintain and administer the buyer-seller relationship.

It is necessary that the salesman working with a specific prospect both determine at what stage in the decision process the prospect is working and lay plans for moving the organizational buyer from one stage to the next. Knowing the stage of the decision process at a given time helps in two ways. First, it provides important clues about the participants in the decision process at that time; second, it suggests the kinds of information that will be most useful to buying influencers.

Like the other parts of the communication mix, the salesman is not a passive agent in the buying process, responding to the prospective customer's information requirements. He can be instrumental in *initiating* any and all stages of the decision process. He can help identify need, for example, by demonstrating the superior performance of his product in order to show why the organizational buyer should be dissatisfied with his present level of goal attainment. He can be especially influential in helping to develop specifications, hoping for a specification that favors his company's products. He can convince the gatekeepers and other influencers that they have identified a sufficiently wide variety of alternatives to proceed to evaluation. And so on.

The objective of organizational marketers is to coordinate buying roles and to move the buying center smoothly through the decision process to the conclusive act of selecting him as a supplier. In designing his market-strategies the marketer has to understand the nature of the buying decision process, including the information sources relied upon by the members of the buying center and their criteria for evaluating the alternative buying courses of action.

Information Sources. It is imperative that the marketing strategist know the information sources relied upon by those key buying influentials in his prospective customer organizations. Unfortunately, a simple list seldom gives sufficient understanding of the importance of various sources, inasmuch as the importance of a given information source is likely to vary according to at least four distinct sets of factors: the individual's buying role, the stage in the decision process, the buying situation, and the stage in the product life cycle.

Numerous studies have found that the manufacturer's salesman was regarded as the most valuable source of new product information by industrial buyers, except that trade journal advertising was judged most important in creating simple awareness. For obtaining trial and full-scale product adoption, salesmen were clearly the most influential information source. Buyers and engineers in other companies became more important during "evaluation" (pretrial assessment), but were not as important as salesmen at this stage.[2]

[2] Frederick E. Webster, Jr., "Informal Communication in Industrial Markets," *Journal of Marketing Research*, VII (May 1970), 186–89. Some of these findings are also supported by Urban B. Ozanne and Gilbert A. Churchill, "Adoption Research: Information Sources in the Industrial Purchasing Decision," in Robert L. King, ed., *Marketing and the New Science of Planning* (Chicago: The American Marketing Association, 1968), 352–59.

Organizational buyers make heavy and almost continuous use of catalogues. These are of two kinds: those provided by individual suppliers and those organized by publishers to include as complete a listing as possible of all suppliers and products in a given category. These so-called "prefiled" catalogues sometimes are prepared for particular classes of users, for example, architects, municipal buyers, hospitals, and industrial purchasing agents. The buyer wishing to find a particular product would find virtually all potential suppliers listed in such a catalogue.

Salesmen, media (trade journal) advertising, direct mail, catalogues, acquaintances in other organizations, professional associations, local service clubs, community organizations, and many more information sources provide the organizational buyer with a continual stream of information about products and services and their suppliers. The problem for the marketing strategist is to invest his promotional resources in those information sources that will be most likely to reach and have an impact and influence on the decision processes of those individuals who are most influential in the purchase of his products. A key consideration in the design of promotional strategy is to locate the "gatekeepers" who control the flow of information into the buying organization and to ascertain the information sources which are most important to them.

Criteria for Evaluation.   In designing organizational marketing strategies it is important to identify the personal goals of the members of the buying center, those things that are important to them, and those goals for which they are striving in their buying actions.

In addition to his "formal" goals, those which he derives from the purposes of the organization and his position in it, the individual will have strong personal goals which motivate his behavior in the buying situation.

To determine those things that are important to the individual buying influential, it is often useful to ask him (either in a survey, or more informally as part of the sales call) to talk about those problems that he has to solve. Although inferences about goals which are valid for general marketing strategy often can be based upon an identification of the organizational positions occupied by key buying influentials, these inferences would not be specific enough for the salesman who has to interact with specific individuals. The salesman must be trained to ask questions that will elicit responses revealing the individual's goals and, more importantly, he must be trained to listen carefully and to analyze the responses of prospective customers, using behavioral science concepts of the kind considered in this book. This is neither more nor less than the important step of "identifying buyers' needs" that is often said to be the basis of any effective marketing strategy.

In addition to being determined by his personal goals and those of the organization, the individual's choice among alternative buying actions also will be directed by the application of several other criteria. These criteria may not be as important as goals, but they nonetheless constrain the set of feasible buying alternatives. Among the most obvious criteria are those relating to organizational policies, such as preferences for dealing with local suppliers, policies relating to the audit of vendor operations (as when a financial statement must be submitted by the potential supplier as proof of his ability to provide uninterrupted service), and credit terms required by the customer. Many organizational buyers will not commit themselves to buy materials for which there is only one source of supply, and the availability of selecting sources of equal quality then becomes an important criterion in selecting suppliers. Other criteria often found in organizational buying include a requirement that suppliers provide nearby stocks, have prompt repair service available, and be willing to accept returns of unused or unacceptable merchandise.

These and other task- and nontask-related criteria become conditions that the potential supplier must be able to meet. They may be peculiar to a specific customer (in which case their identification and a response to them is the responsibility of the salesman), or they may be characteristic of a segment of the market.

THE BUYING SITUATION

Every buying situation can be characterized by three interrelated factors:

1. The newness of the problem and the extent to which the key decision-makers have relevant buying experience;
2. The amount and type of information requirements of members of the buying center;
3. The number of new alternatives considered in the buying decision process.

Given these three criteria, buying situations can be classified as new task, straight rebuy, and modified rebuy.[3]

New task buying situations are those which have not arisen before and in which the buyer has little or no relevant past buying experience to draw upon. In such situations a great deal of information is required and new alternatives must be considered to solve the problem.

Straight rebuy situations are recurring buying situations which do not require any new information and are handled on a routine basis. In such situations there is often no motivation to consider new sources of supply.

Modified rebuy situations are those which may develop from either new task or straight rebuy situations. The buying alternatives are known but they are changed (e.g., a price change or any other change in any of the supplier's offerings) and buyers have some relevant buying experience although some additional information is needed and new sources of supply may be considered.

[3] Patrick J. Robinson, Charles W. Faris, and Yoram Wind, *Industrial Buying and Creative Marketing* (Boston: Allyn & Bacon, Inc., 1967).

There is some evidence to suggest that these situations lead to somewhat different decision-making processes (extended versus limited versus habitual) and behavioral responses. The three buying situations, coupled with the position of the marketing organization as an "in" or "out" supplier, can provide a useful basis for organizational market segmentation and guidelines for the design of organizational marketing strategies.[4]

FACTORS AFFECTING THE BUYING DECISION

The buyers' predispositions, preferences, and decision models can serve as surrogate measures of the environmental, organizational, interpersonal, and individual variables affecting the buyers' response to marketing stimuli.

Prevailing loyalties and attitudes toward and preference among brands and suppliers define the problems and the opportunities facing the marketer. The present predispositions of buying influencers toward the marketer's company, products, and services also define the marketing task. Knowing the loyalties, attitudes, and preferences of buyers is as important as understanding their needs and goals in defining the challenges facing the marketer. The perceived risk model identifies loyalty to suppliers as an important risk-reducing strategy and suggests at the same time that any attempt to induce buyers to change suppliers may be preceived as threatening by some of them.

The marketing strategist can deepen his understanding of potential customers by using the perceived risk model as an aid in defining the key concerns of the decision process. To do this, the strategist must understand the major uncertainties in the mind of the decision-maker. What is this buyer's characteristic strategy for reducing risk: loyalty, avoidance, information seeking, or investment reduction? What are the constraints on the amount of time, effort, and money available for this buying decision? Where does he feel uncomfortable in making judgments? Is he more concerned about the reactions of other people (psychosocial risk) or about product performance?

It is important to remember, for organizational buying behavior at least as much as for consumer behavior, that the key uncertainties causing perceived risk often relate to the reactions of other people, not to product performance. The marketer's major problem in stimulating an order from a prospective customer may be to convince the decider that the course of action he is recommending will be acceptable to other influencers.

The major reason for defining perceived risk and identifying the various attributes which determine the buyers' choice behavior is, of course, to identify the information that will be most useful to potential buyers in reducing perceived risk and stimulating buying action.

---

[4] For a detailed discussion of the marketing strategy implications of the three buying situations see Robinson, Faris, and Wind, *op. cit.*, Chapter XIII.

Developing Marketing Strategies

Despite the distinguishing characteristics of organizational markets, conceptually there should be no difference in the marketing management approach to organizational markets and to consumer markets. The specific variables affecting the organizational buyer's response to marketing strategies differ, of course, from those affecting the household buying decisions; similarly, the importance and degree of utilization of various marketing strategies (e.g., personal versus impersonal communication) differ significantly between organizational and consumer markets. Yet the basic marketing decisions, the approach that should be utilized in making the decisions (e.g., explicit, formal procedures), and the tools that should be employed in making them (e.g., marketing research, quantitative analytical techniques) are basically identical to those utilized by sophisticated modern marketing management of consumer products.

This basic premise suggests that effective organizational marketing management requires primarily an understanding of the modern analytical approach to marketing management and of the characteristics and determinants of organizational buying behavior.[5]

Following this approach, the remainder of this chapter is devoted to a discussion of the three major sets of marketing decisions:

1. Identification of appropriate market segments;
2. Determination of the organizational marketing mix;
3. Management of the marketing function.

IDENTIFICATION OF APPROPRIATE MARKET SEGMENTS

Organizational Market Segmentation.[6]   Organizational markets can be segmented into "macro" segments based on organizational characteristics. Then, within each macrosegment, the market can be further subdivided into "micro" segments, based on the characteristics of the relevant decision-making unit.

At both levels of segmentation two types of bases for segmentation are distinguished—viz., general and situation-specific characteristics. At the micro level the general and situation-specific characteristics are the same as in consumer segmentation. At the macro level, however, the general characteristics are certain characteristics intrinsic to the organization, such as geographic location and size, which affect the general character of de-

---

[5] An excellent example of the analytic approach can be found in Philip Kotler, *Marketing Management: Analysis, Planning, and Control* (Englewood Cliffs, N.J.: Prentice-Hall, Inc., 1967).

[6] This section has been drawn, in part, from Ronald E. Frank, William F. Massy, and Yoram Wind, *Market Segmentation* (Englewood Cliffs, N.J.: Prentice-Hall, Inc., 1971).

mand—the types of goods purchased, the way in which they are purchased, and so on. Situation-specific organization characteristics are those related to the interaction between the organization and the given product, supplier, or purchase situation. The various bases for organization segmentation are depicted in Table 8–2.

General Organizational Characteristics. The general organizational chracteristics of primary importance in segmenting organizational markets are organizational demographics and the nature of the organization task, structure, and technology.

"Organizational demographics," such as size, Standard Industrial Classification category, end use of product, and geographical location, are frequently used as bases for segmentation. Cardozo, in his review of the industrial segmentation literature, concludes that "In these publications market segmentation is seldom carried further than stating that, for any particular industrial product, purchasing behavior varies according to geographic and end use of the commodity purchased. End use is generally thought to vary directly with the type of business in which the business firm is engaged." [7]

The most popular basis for industrial segmentation is the Standard Industrial Classification (SIC), which has been adopted by the Federal Government and most state governments as a basis for collecting and presenting statistical data relating to business firms. A number of industrial companies have geared their sales and marketing efforts to the SIC system.

The specific nature of the organization—its task, structure, technology, and members—and the idiosyncratic interaction among these factors and between them and the external environment are important determinants of organizational buying decisions. Salesmen have often used these factors as indicators of the type of organization they confront, although no systematic use of these factors as bases for segmentation has been undertaken. Conceptually, however, one can segment organizations in terms of their tasks, structure, and technology.

Situation-Specific Organizational Characteristics. Classifying organizational customers on the basis of their usage of a given product (heavy versus light users) is a frequent practice of industrial marketers. Yet product usage is only one of a number of possible situation-specific bases for organizational segmentation. The degree of source loyalty, the nature of the buying center, the specific buying situation, the attitudes, perceptions, and preferences of the members of the buying center toward the source of supply, its products, and personnel, and the determinants of the buying decision and their relative importance are all possible bases for segmentation.

One of the authors investigated the degree and correlates of source loyalty in the purchase of industrial components by a West Coast elec-

[7] Richard N. Cardozo, "Segmenting the Industrial Market," in Robert L. King, ed., *Marketing and the New Science of Planning* (Chicago: American Marketing Association, 1968), 433–40.

TABLE 8-2   A Classification Scheme of Bases for Organizational
Segmentation

Type of Measure by (Object)		Nature of Characteristics	
		General Characteristics	Situation Specific Characteristics
Organizational Characteristics	Objective Measures	Organization Demographics: SIC category, geographic location. Organization Structure & Technology	Product Usage Loyalty Pattern The Buying Center Buying Situation
	Inferred Measures	Buying tasks and Purchasing Decision Rules	Attitudes, Perception and Preference The Determinants of the Purchase Decision and Their Relative Importance
DMU Characteristics *	Objective Measures	Demographic Characteristics: Age, Sex, Education	Loyalty Pattern
	Inferred Measures	Personality and Life Style	Attitudes, Perception and Preference

* Decision Making Unit

Source: Ronald E. Frank, William F. Massy, and Yoram Wind, Market Segmentation (Englewood Cliffs, N.J.: Prentice-Hall, Inc., 1971).

tronics firm.[8] His findings reveal a very high degree of source loyalty for both fabricated and standard industrial components. If the degree of source loyalty varies from one organization to another—a likely assumption —it can serve as a basis for segmentation.

DMU Characteristics. Once markets have been segmented at the macro-organizational level, they can then be further subdivided by the characteristics of the key decision-making units within each organization— for example, by age, education, professional affiliation, personality, and attitudes. The appropriate bases for segmentation within macrosegments may be the same across all macrosegments or may differ. The particular DMU characteristics are basically the ones discussed in Chapter 7. They include both general characteristics (e.g., personality, age, sex, education) and situation specific characteristics (e.g., attitudes, loyalty pattern) similar to the ones used as bases for segmentation of consumer markets.[9]

[8] Yoram Wind, "Industrial Source Loyalty," *Journal of Marketing Research,* VII (November 1970), 450–57.

[9] For a detailed discussion of the various bases for consumer and organization segmentation and of the concepts, theory, and research approaches to segmentation, see Frank, Massy, and Wind, *op. cit.*

The relevance of the various alternative bases for segmentation, at both the macro (organizational) and DMU levels, depends to a large extent on the particular product or service considered. In any specific case the appropriate base or bases will depend on the nature of the given product or service, the firm's objectives and constraints, the potential size of the segment, the ease of its measurement, its accessibility (through media and channels of distribution), and the cost of reaching it. Unfortunately, there are only a few studies of any direct relevance for identifying and evaluating alternative bases for organizational segmentation.

A number of possible bases for segmentation were suggested in this section, but the appropriateness of each of them should be assessed in each situation. Furthermore, since the costs of defining and reaching a market segment is in many cases prohibitive, research should be directed not only toward identifying the relevant characteristics of the macro (organizational) and micro (DMU) segments, but also toward evaluating the cost and benefits anticipated from segmenting on a given base or combination of bases.

DETERMINATION OF THE ORGANIZATIONAL MARKETING MIX

Effective organizational marketing strategies require both the tailoring of the product, price, distribution, and promotion strategies to the needs of the target market segments and the desired product positioning. The selection of appropriate market segments is based, in turn, on knowledge of organizational buying behavior. In other words, in deciding on the mix of marketing strategies with the highest probability of leading toward the most effective and efficient marketing practice, the marketing managers of a firm whose customers are formal organizations must take explicit account of the behavior of the buyers and the intermediate channels (which can also be viewed as organizational buyers) which they utilize. Similarly, a distributor or any other intermediate marketing organization which is planning marketing strategy also must take explicit account of his buyers' behavior and must design his strategies to best meet the needs of his market segments.

As indicated earlier, the *approach* for making organizational marketing decisions does not differ from the one utilized in consumer markets, although the specific nature of the product, price, promotion, and distribution strategies and the relative importance of each of these components in the ultimate marketing mix does vary.[10]

[10] Not only is there conceptually no difference between the type of organizational and consumer marketing decisions and the approach that should be utilized in making them, but a comparison of existing industrial marketing texts with general marketing management texts reveals few idiosyncratic "industrial" characteristics in any of the industrial texts. Actually, if one were to delete the word industrial from the chapters in industrial marketing texts dealing with product, price, promotion, and distribution decisions, the chapters could very well be ascribed to any general marketing management text. For example, see some of the current industrial marketing texts: Lawrence Fisher, *Industrial Marketing: An Analytical Ap-*

Product and Service Mix. A company's product and service mix is its primary vehicle for achieving its objectives regarding profits, sales stability, sales growth, and image. This requires an optimal product mix reflecting the company's response to changing opportunities and resources. Product and service decisions are concerned with the positioning, introduction, modification, and deletion of products. Determining the desired (and actual) positioning of a product, a product line, or a product mix *vis-à-vis* its competitors for each of the relevant market segments provides guidelines for the design of the product and service offerings, as well as for the other elements of the marketing mix.

The nature and positioning of any product mix aimed at organizational customers is affected, however, by two idiosyncratic characteristics of organizational buying—the buyer's need for services, and the importance of the technical ability of the supplying company. In addition, because organizational buying is determined by both task- and nontask-related variables, any product design or modification should focus not only on functional features but also on style and other nontask-related elements.

The organizational buyer often requires a variety of commercial and product support services, especially prompt emergency delivery and reliable, planned future delivery. The delivery requirement is often tied in with the buyer's stock decision and the supplier's willingness to carry the stock for the buyers. Product support service before, during, and after the sale is an extremely important component of the product mix a company can offer. By providing before-sales service, a marketer can help the buying organization with technical assistance, advice, and information at all the stages of the buying decision process. This assistance, whether aimed at the identification of a problem or the formulation of product specification, provides the buyer with valuable service. At the same time it also increases the supplier's chances of being selected to provide the product or service he helped specify.

The objectives and role of technical service, in the context of the product-service mix, must be carefully thought out by the marketer. Simon, for example, classified service objectives into sales objectives, such as broadening the available market, maintaining an account, and contributing to the reputation of the company; product performance objectives, such as extending the output life of the customer's equipment, getting the product to perform to specifications, obtaining feedback on the quality and acceptability of the product, and teaching and helping the customer to use the product; and nonsales competitive objectives, such as obtaining feedback on competitor's equipment and keeping abreast of the customer's needs.[11]

---

proach to Planning and Execution (New York: Brandon Systems Press, 1970); Ralph S. Alexander, James S. Cross, and Richard M. Hill, *Industrial Marketing* (Homewood, Ill.: Richard D. Irwin, Inc., 1967); H. Robert Dodge, *Industrial Marketing* (New York: McGraw-Hill Book Company, 1970); Aubrey Wilson, *The Marketing of Industrial Products* (London: Hutchinson & Co., Ltd., 1965).

[11] L. S. Simon, "Measuring the Marketing Impact of Technical Services," *Journal of Marketing Research*, II (February 1965).

In most organizational buying situations, the supplier's ability to solve the buyer's current and future needs is an important consideration in the selection of a given supplier. The supplier's research and development activities and production facilities are frequently examined by the buying organization. Yet, most frequently, the most important component of the supplier's capabilities are the personnel available, their skills, creativity, and willingness to interact and help the buying organization.

Price Decisions. Despite the growing emphasis on nonprice variables, setting a price, initiating a price change, and responding to competitors' price changes are among the most important marketing decisions. In determining the firm's price strategy, four sets of factors have to be considered: (1) the effect of the price on the other marketing mix elements (the nature of the product, and the type and amount of advertising and distribution) and especially on the customer's perceived product quality and value; (2) the cost of producing and marketing the product; (3) customer's price elasticities; and (4) competitor's actions and probable reactions.

The solicitation of competitive bids is a common practice in organizational buying. Because the preparation of bids is expensive and time consuming for the marketer, it is important to have an initial assessment of the likelihood of winning the sale and the potential value of the order as a basis for deciding whether to submit a bid. A preliminary review of the buying situation can help in this assessment.

In pricing decisions, understanding the organizational buyer's sensitivity to prices and the importance of price in determining the buying decisions is a crucial input to the design of an "optimum" price strategy.

Personal Selling. For several reasons the salesman in organizational marketing is the key marketing resource. First, he can identify those individuals within the organization who influence the decision process and their goals. Because the composition of the buying center varies significantly from one organization to another and from one buying situation to another, generalizations about the nature of the buying decision process are likely to be inadequate as bases for the development of marketing strategy. Instead, the salesman on the spot must identify those specific individuals and their specific goals in the particular buying situation. Only then is there a basis for an effective marketing presentation.

Second, the organizational buyer requires specific information showing how the supplier's products can satisfy his needs. Mass media and impersonal sources of information cannot provide the kind of precisely tailored information that is necessary to reduce the product performance and psychosocial risk that specific individuals within the buying center perceive in the buying situation.

Third, as a form of communication, personal selling has the distinct advantage of providing immediate and direct feedback to the communicator (the salesman) in the form of the buying influencer's responses to his messages. This feedback helps the communicator to assess on the spot his effectiveness in obtaining his objectives and allows for immediate adjustment of the message to more precisely meet the influencer's needs and predispositions.

The complexity and the size of organizational buying units, and the significant differences among them, explain why personal selling is a major marketing tool in such markets. Whereas consumer goods marketers can define marketing segmentation strategies based upon reliable profiles of a few rather distinct consumer types, the marketer selling to formal organizations finds it much more difficult to define large market segments. Rather, organizational marketing strategies often take the form of "key account" strategies—that is, specific plans for working with each of the many organizations that are potential customers. Such effort is necessary because of the uniqueness of each buying situation and it is economically feasible because of the larger dollar amounts involved in most organizational purchases compared with consumer marketing. It is somewhat ironic that the millions of potential buyers for many consumer products can be approached as several distinct market segments of several hundred thousand consumers each, but that the few hundred buyers that constitute most organizational market segments must be approached within the segments on a more or less individualistic basis.

The important role of personal selling in organizational marketing requires special attention to the various sales force decisions. These decisions concerning the setting of sales force objectives, recruiting, selection, and training of salesmen, determining the size of the sales force, organizing, directing, compensating, and controlling it are all decisions that have to be made in light of the requirements of the salesman's job and its role vis-à-vis the organizational buying process.[12]

For example, the fact that the organizational buying process is carried out by various members of a buying center may suggest organizing the marketing staff in groups of specialists around a salesman—an "account executive" who coordinates the efforts of the marketing team. Such a team can service the various decision points in the customer's buying process. Each member of the team would be responsible for developing and maintaining close working and personal relationships with his counterparts in the buying organization.

Advertising, Sales Promotion, and Publicity. Despite the dominant position of personal selling in the communication system of companies whose customers are formal organizations, advertising, sales promotion, and publicity are still important parts of this system. The primary objective of organizational advertising is frequently viewed as that of playing a supporting role to the sales force. Specific advertising campaign objectives will be stronger to the extent that they are based upon a careful appraisal of characteristic buying situations, including the composition of the buying center and the nature of the individual decision-maker's predispositions.

---

[12] For detailed discussion of these decisions see Kenneth R. Davis and Frederick E. Webster, Jr., *Sales Force Management* (New York: The Ronald Press, 1968); and Charles S. Goodman, *Management of the Personal Selling Function* (New York: Holt, Rinehart & Winston, Inc., 1971).

Likewise, the design of the advertising message and the selection of advertising media require fairly detailed information on buyer characteristics.

Assuming that the organizational buyer is a "rational," "economic man" motivated by profit motive rather than by personal gratification has led many advertisers and scholars to believe that "rational appeals must be stressed instead of the emotional ones often so effective in consumer advertising." [13] Yet the fact that nontask variables play an important role in determining organizational buying behavior suggests the need to avoid generalizations of this sort and to design the advertising message in each case on the basis of the characteristics of the members of the buying center (personality, attitudes, etc.), the policies and nature of the organization (size, objectives, etc.), the objectives of the advertising campaign and its relation to the sales force plan, and the particular characteristics of the product/service to be advertised.

Media reaching organizational buyers are quite distinct from the general media reaching consumer markets, with business and trade publications being the primary media used by organizational advertisers. These include special industry publications (e.g., *World Oil, Aviation Week and Space Technology*) professional publications (e.g., *Purchasing, Purchasing Week, Chemical Engineering*), and general business publications (e.g., *Business Week, Fortune, The Wall Street Journal*). A unique feature of many of the industry and professional publications is their reader service cards—postcard inserts for use by readers who are interested in further information.

Catalogues, brochures, and specification sheets provide reference material for the members of organizational buying centers (purchasing, engineering, and office personnel), and together with direct mail comprise another important medium used to reach organizational buyers.

Exhibits, trade shows, and displays are the major sales promotion activities of many organizational marketers.[14] The objectives of such shows and exhibits are to meet potential customers, make direct sales, build prospect lists, discover new applications for existing products, introduce new products, demonstrate nonportable equipment, meet competitive effort, hire personnel, and establish new representatives, dealers, or suppliers.[15] An understanding of the nature of the organizational market is a prime factor in determining which show to participate in and how to organize the exhibit.

Distribution of free *samples*, another commonly used sales promotion technique, requires similar awareness and understanding of the organizational buying process. Samples of electronic components given to research and development personnel, for example, were found to be extremely

[13] Ralph S. Alexander, James S. Cross, and Richard M. Hill, *Industrial Marketing*, 3rd ed. (Homewood, Illinois: Richard D. Irwin, Inc., 1967), 409.

[14] For a detailed allocation of the advertising budget among the various media for a sample of industrial firms, see the "Annual Survey of Industrial Advertising Budgets" which is published annually by *Industrial Marketing*.

[15] For a detailed discussion of these objectives, see Alexander, Cross, and Hill, *op. cit.*, 434–38.

effective selling devices because the R&D engineers used them in the design of new prototype products. The same samples when given to other members of the organization (in this case, purchasing personnel) had very limited effect.[16]

Entertainment of customers is still a common form of sales promotion. Yet whether or not to entertain, who should be entertained (the purchasing agent, the user, or the influencer), and who should entertain (a salesman, a marketing vice president) depend primarily on the specific buying circumstances and the importance of task versus nontask determinants of the buying process.

Publicity most commonly takes the form of articles in trade journals. Given the higher credibiltiy of this source of information, the marketer explicitly should plan his publicity campaign so as to aim it at the key buying influencers who may respond most favorably to this form of promotion.

Distribution Mix. The most important determinants of whether to design a channel of distribution around the company's own sales force, distributors, manufacturer's agents and sales agents, brokers, manufacturer's branch houses, or any combination of these intermediaries, are the characteristics and needs of the buying organizations to be served. These characteristics include the number of customers in the desired market segment, their geographical distribution, purchase frequency, average quantity bought, frequency of straight rebuy versus new task situations, purchase preferences, susceptibility to different selling methods, and especially their specific needs.

The Organizational Marketing Mix. The nature of organizational buying as reflected in the idiosyncratic characteristics of the product, price, promotion, and distribution decisions of firms whose customers are formal organizations suggests an organizational marketing mix in which the emphasis is primarily on product service and personal selling. This conclusion is further supported by a study designed to identify the key policies common to successful marketing managements.[17]

MANAGEMENT OF THE MARKETING FUNCTION

Marketing management is the analyzing, organizing, planning, and controlling of the firm's customer-impinging resources, policies, and activities (marketing mix) with a view to satisfying the needs and wants of chosen customer groups at a profit.[18] This definition explicitly and implicitly encompasses four interrelated elements of the marketing management process

[16] Yoram Wind, "Industrial Buying Behavior: Source Loyalty of Industrial Components," unpublished Ph.D. dissertation, Graduate School of Business, Stanford University, 1966.

[17] Jon G. Udell, "How Important is Pricing in Competitive Strategy?" *Journal of Marketing,* XXVIII (January 1964), 44–48.

[18] Kotler, *op. cit.,* 12.

which are common to firms whose customers are formal organizations and firms whose customers are households:

1. The primary objective of marketing management is to create customer satisfaction subject to the achievement of the firm's own objectives;

2. The marketing decisions of the firm should be tailored to the needs of chosen market segments; hence the need to analyze the market, understand customer behavior, and decide on the desired market segments;

3. The marketing mix is seen as a synergistic system composed of the firm's marketing decisions.

4. The management of marketing includes the administrative activities of analysis, organization, planning, and control and involves directing all parts of the business toward the primary objective of creating a satisfied customer.

The idiosyncratic characteristics of organizational marketing as reflected in the selection of target markets and design of the marketing mix (elements 2 and 3) were discussed in the previous sections. In setting the marketing objectives and managing the marketing function (elements 1 and 4) management has to follow the same procedures and use the same tools as management of any consumer goods firm. However, marketing decisions, like buying decisions, are being made in the context of a formal organization and are therefore quite likely to be affected by the same basic forces as affect organizational buying (environmental, organizational, interpersonal, and personal task and nontask factors). Hence, an understanding of organizational buying behavior may make the marketing manager whose customers are formal organizations more sensitive to the forces affecting decisions in his own organization and more effective and efficient as a manager.

Systematic attempts to understand the organizational buying process are likely to improve significantly the effectiveness and efficiency of marketing strategies aimed at organizational buyers. Yet, because most marketing decisions have to take into account other variables (such as the firm's objectives and constraints, and the characteristics and actions of the other participants in the marketing system—e.g., competitors, intermediaries, government, etc.), understanding organizational buying behavior can be considered as a necessary but not sufficient condition for successful marketing strategy. To increase the usefulness of factual information about the buying process it must be combined with a viable conceptual knowledge about the nature of organizational buying behavior. Any attempt to apply conceptual knowledge of organizational buying behavior to the design of marketing strategies requires, however, specific information derived from marketing research. Increasingly, the question that confronts marketing managers of firms whose customers are formal organizations is not whether organizational buying behavior should be studied, but how to best study it. Organizational buying research, as an integral part of organizational marketing research, can be defined as systematic model-building, data-gathering, analysis, and interpretation for the purpose of improved decision making in the marketing of organizational goods and services.

If published studies represent actual practice, little effort has been devoted to the scientific study of organizational buying behavior. Conceptually, there is no justification for this fact. Organizational buying behavior models, such as the one proposed in this book, can be utilized as guidelines for research. Secondary and primary data collection procedures can be employed and analytical techniques such as multivariate statistical techniques and multidimensional scaling analyses can be utilized in the study of organizational buying behavior.

The results of the few available studies are encouraging enough to lead us to believe that future research on organizational buying behavior will utilize to a much greater extent these and other available research procedures coupled with the construction of models of relevant interactive systems.

Summary

The main theme of this book has been that whereas organizational marketing management is similar in approach to consumer marketing management, organizational buying behavior differs distinctly from consumer behavior and requires explicit analysis and concern. Models of consumer behavior cannot serve, therefore, as a substitute for organizational buying models.

Most of the recent consumer behavior models are decision process models which emphasize the essential rationality of consumer decision processes, in contrast to an earlier emphasis upon the ego-defensive and status seeking aspects of buyer behavior. At the same time, our general model of organizational buying behavior suggests that it is useful to consider the important psychological and interpersonal aspects of individual decision-making behavior, which may be obscured in suprarational views of organizational decision making.

At another level of analysis, the organization itself must be seen as a decision-making unit. It both constrains and integrates the decisions of individuals. Therefore, to consider only individual decision making without looking also at the influence of such factors as information flows and authority structures within the organization is to make an incomplete appraisal of the organizational buying process.

How, then, does organizational buying behavior differ from consumer behavior? What *caveats* must be heeded in applying theories of consumer behavior to the study of organizational buyers? First, seldom does one individual have sole responsibility and authority for the buying decision. Second, organizational buying behavior is motivated by a complex combination of individual and organizational needs and objectves. Third, the formal organization provides an important context within which information flows and is processed. Fourth, the organizational decision process is likely to be more *explicit*, as a reflection of the need for the several members of the buying center to coordinate their activities and to obey the policies and control procedures of the organization. This observation is consistent with the observation that the organizational decision process is a *rational* one, for it is the explicitness of the buying decision process which permits the identification of stages in the decision process and makes it possible to identify more or less clearly the involvement of the several buying roles at various stages.

For these reasons, models of consumer behavior are likely to be incomplete as descriptions of organizational buying behavior, because they leave out the influence of the formal organization and some of the essential characteristics of the buying process. At the same time, they *are* valid descriptions of the buying decision processes followed by individuals within the context of the formal organization. Thus, although this argument suggests the need for the development of organizational buying models, general models such as the one proposed in this book still require further transformation into problem-specific models. Such models can be verified empirically and, with the aid of the general organizational buying model, can improve the effectiveness of the marketing manager's decisions by improving the accuracy of his predictions of how organizational buyers respond to his marketing efforts, and by suggesting guidelines for the design of marketing strategies tailored to the needs of organizational buyers.

INDEX

Thompson, J. D., 41
Tosi, H. L., 18
Trade associations, 48-49
Tulman, E. C., 89

Udell, J. G., 125
Users, 78

Values, 51

Walton, R. E., 84

Warshofsky, F., 49
Webster, F. E., Jr., 5, 11, 20, 22, 30, 50, 51, 72, 73, 113, 123
Weigand, R. E., 19
Wiener, A. J., 49
Wilson, A., 121
Wilson, D. T., 91, 105
Wind, Y., 11, 15, 24-26, 37, 38, 66, 72, 81, 106, 115-17, 119, 125
Work flow, 60-61